spiz-neak
(speak)

a secret language your parents and teachers won't understand

Jim Wagner

First printing: May 2015

spiz-neak
a secret language your parents and teachers won't understand

TM & © 2015 by Jim Wagner
Printed in the United States of America

Published by **WAR**Arts
P.O. Box 15133
Irvine, California 92628-5113 USA
www.jimwagnerrealitybased.com

ISBN: 978-0-9863269-3-6

Illustrations by Tammy DiGiacomo

This book is dedicated to
Darya, Yasmin, Sanam,
Gary and Manique
(the first ones to learn modern spiz-neak)
alright, and you too Amanda and Vartan,
who are "big kids"

TABLE OF CONTENTS

(tiz-nable iz-nof ciz-non|tiz-nents)

spiz-neak is actually the word "speak." It is a language, based on splitting up and modifying English words, that your parents, teachers, and unwanted listeners won't understand when you are speaking it with those in your inner circle.

spiz-neak is a spoken language. Of course it can be written, like any language, but if you write it down on paper, or text it, then it becomes easy for others to decipher (understand the meaning) how the language works, and then it will no longer be a secret. However, when spiz-neak is spoken, and in short bursts just enough to communicate your message to your siblings or friends in the know, then it is almost impossible for outsiders to pick it up by just listening to it. Even if somebody, like your least favorite teacher at school, learns the basics from this book, will they practice it enough to become fluent? If they are not constantly speaking spiz-neak, like any foreign language, they'll probably only be able to pick out a word or two of what you are saying, but it's unlikely they'll grasp the entire meaning of your sentences. That's the beauty of spiz-neak – to speak your own secret language, and it takes so little time to learn it.

Since so very few people speak spiz-neak in the English-speaking world you will be part of a very exclusive society. The first person to introduce spiz-neak to a friend is called a "speak founder," or in spiz-neak, a **spiz-neak fiz-noun|diz-ner**. Perhaps you are the first person in your family or school to learn spiz-neak and introduce it someone else. In the back of the book there is a speak founder certificate that you and the first person you introduced to spiz-neak are to sign. It becomes your official document that is dated. When three to six people who know each other finally have the ability to to communicate in spiz-neak (although it does not have to be fluent or the lingua franca - a good phrase to look up - that replaces English each time you get together) that is called a "speak club" or more accurately a **spiz-neak cliz-nub**. Once each member knows the 8 Rules of spiz-neak they may sign their name on that certificate, which is also in the back of the book under CERTIFICATES. When there are 10 people or more people that communicate with each other in spiz-neak in the same school, or in the neighborhood, that is known as a "speak group," or **spiz-neak griz-noup**. That is the highest level you can go, and it is quite an accomplishment. It shows real leadership from the founder. Any group over 10 people in the same school or neighborhood is known as a "speak community," **spiz-neak ciz-nom|miz-nuni|tiz-ny**, but there is no certificate for that. It just means that your club became very successful, or there were a lot of other like-minded people in your area with the same idea at the same time.

So, let's get started and learn how to speak spiz-neak with just 8 simple rules.

SINGLE SYLLABLE WORDS

Rule Number 1:
Spiltting single syllable English words to make spiz-neak words

For words that start with a consonant, followed by a vowel, take the first letter of a single syllable word and add the sound *iz* (pronounced exactly like the English word is) after it. Then place the letter *n* before the remaining letters of the word.

Example:
The word **yes** becomes *yiz-nes*. It becomes essentially a two-syllable word. The spiz-neak word is pronounced fast with only the slightest pause between the newly formed syllables; just enough pause so the listener who understands spiz-neak can figure out the word communicated to them.

> **no** becomes *niz-no*
> **car** becomes *ciz-nar*
> **book** becomes *biz-nook*
> **pen** becomes *piz-nen*
> **bike** becomes *biz-nike*

MULTI-SYLLABLE WORDS

Rule Number 2:
Spiltting multi-syllable English words to make spiz-neak words

Two syllable words are divided in between the syllables, indicated with the vertical bar symbol |, and then the spiz-neak extensions are added accordingly. Take the first syllable and add the sound iz after it. In written form the Hyphen, Minus or Dash symbol – is shown after *iz*. Then place the letter *n* before the remaining letters of the first syllable. Repeat the process for the second syllable.

Example:
The word police becomes piz-no|liz-nice. It becomes essentially a four-syllable word. The spiz-neak word is pronounced fast with only the slightest pause between syllables.

> The word **talent** becomes *tiz-nal|liz-nent*
> The word **retreat** becomes *riz-ne|triz-neat*
> The word **glasses** become *gliz-nas|siz-nes*
> The word **toilet** becomes *tiz-noi|liz-net*

For words that have three or more syllable the rule stays the same. Divide the English word according to the syllables, indicated with the vertical bar symbol |, and take the first letter of each syllable and place the sound *iz* after it (in written form the dash symbol – is shown). Then place the letter *n* in front of the remaining letters.

Example:
The word **basketball** becomes *biz-nas|kiz-net|biz-nall*. Yes, it is hard to say this spiz-neak word at first, especially fast, but like any new language it becomes smoother the more it is practiced.

The word **understand** becomes *iz-nunder|stiz-nand*. All words that start with the letters *un* are automatically attached to the first syllable, as you will discover in Rule Number 6, and separated from there like this word as indicated by Rule Number 2.

Rule Number 3:
Stand-alone vowels in between syllables

If a vowel stands alone after a word is divided into syllables then no extension is added it, and it is sandwiched between two vertical symbols |a|.

Example:
The word **paragraph** becomes *piz-nar|a|griz-naph*
The word **tropical** becomes *triz-nop|i|ciz-nal*

An exception to this rule is sometimes the letters "en" that is found in the middle of a word standing alone.

Example:
The word **seventy** becomes *siz-nev|en|tiz-ny*

Rule Number 4:
Words beginning with consonant pairs

The following consonant combinations that begin a word cannot be divided, and the *iz* sound is placed after the two letters listed here:

bl br ch cl cr dr gr fr pr sh sm sp spr st th thr tr wh

Example:
> The word **blue** becomes *bliz-nue*
> The word **brave** becomes *briz-nave*
> The word **chair** becomes *chiz-nair*
> The word **clap** becomes *cliz-nap*
> The word **crack** becomes *criz-nack*
> The word **drew** becomes *driz-new*
> The word **great** becomes *griz-nate*
> The name **Frank** becomes *friz-nank* (in spiz-neak you do not capitalize words)
> The word *pride* becomes *priz-nide*
> The word **shy** becomes *shiz-ny* with the *ny* pronounced *nigh*.
> The word **small** becomes *smiz-nall*
> The word **sport** becomes *spiz-nort*
> The word **spring** becomes *spriz-ning*
> The word **stop** becomes *stiz-nop*
> The word **this** becomes *thiz-nis*
> The word **trick** becomes *triz-nick*

The word **through** becomes *thriz-nough*

The word **what** becomes **whiz-nat**. The *at* still has the same sound as the original English word.

Rule Number 5:
Words beginning with a vowel

For single syllable words that start with a vowel, followed by a consonant, you must start the entire new spiz-neak word with the **iz** sound. Then you place the letter n in front of the entire original English word.

Example:

The word **are** becomes ***iz-nare***. There is only a slight pause between the letter "z" and the letter "n." Pronunciation must be clear, and like any new language you learn you must start off speaking slowly, and get faster with confidence.

>**all** becomes ***iz-nall***
>**art** becomes ***iz-art***
>**at** becomes ***iz-at***
>**eye** becomes ***iz-neye***
>**ice** becomes ***iz-nice***

Rule Number 6:
Words beginning with a vowel and consonant pair

The following two letters must remain together, and the ***iz-n*** sound is placed before them:

af an un im in

The two letters af before a word not only has ***iz-n*** placed before it, but the ***af*** stays attached to the syllable after it.

Example:

>The word **after** becomes ***iz-naf|tiz-ner***
>The word **angry** becomes ***iz-nan|griz-ny***, with the ***ny***

pronounced *nee*.

The two letters un before a word not only has iz-n placed before it, but the un stays attached to the syllable after it.

Exampe:

> The word **under** becomes *iz-nunder*
> The word **until** becomes *iz-nuntil*
> The word **unclear** becomes *iz-nunclear*
> The word **unloved** becomes *iz-nunloved*
> The word **understand** becomes *iz-nunder|stiz-nand*
> The word **unimpressed** becomes *iz-nunim|priz-nessed*
> The word **uneducated** becomes *iz-nuned|u|ciz-nated*
>
> The word **impossible** becomes *iz-nimpos|siz-nible*
> The word **immediate** becomes *iz-nimme|diz-niate*

Again, this rule is also for the two letters in before a word. For all words beginning with **in** the sound *iz-n* goes before it, and the **in** stays attached to the syllable after it.

Example:

> The word **inactive** becomes *iz-ninac|tiz-nive*
> The word **inappropriate** becomes *iz-ninap|priz-no|priz-niate*

Rule Number 7:
Words ending with consonant pairs

The following word endings must stay together at the end of the last consonant:

en (with an exception) **es** **le** **ion** **ing** **ish**

Example:

> The word **eleven** becomes *iz-ne|liz-neven*, because **en** is the last syllable
> The word **heaven** becomes *hiz-nea|viz-nen*, because **en**

is actually with the letter **v** making the last syllable *ven*

The word **dishes** becomes *diz-nishes*
The word **wishes** becomes *wiz-nishes*
The words ***Los Angeles*** becomes *liz-nos iz-nangeles*, because it also falls under Rule Numbers 6 and 8

The word **little** becomes *liz-nittle*
The word **principle** becomes *priz-nin/ciz-niple*
The word **double** becomes *diz-nouble*

The word **mission** becomes *miz-nission*
The word **revolution** becomes *riz-nev/o/liz-nution*
The word **constitution** becomes *ciz-non/stiz-ni/tiz-nu tion*

The word **hiking** becomes *hiz-niking*
The word **swimming** becomes *swiz-nimming*
The word **talking** becomes *tiz-nalking*

The word **foolish** becomes *fiz-noolish*
The word **polish** becomes *piz-nolish*
The word **Spanish** becomes *spiz-nanish*

Rule Number 8:
Unusual or foreign words

If you come across a word not covered in the first seven rules, such an unusual English word or a foreign word, then the rule is to make that word a spiz-neak word the best you can. As long as everyone in your inner circle understands that word that you are trying to communicate then you have accomplished the goal.

Now you know all of the rules for spiz-neak.

NOUN

A noun is a person, place, or thing.

Example:
>The word **man** becomes *miz-nan*
>The word **woman** becomes *wiz-no/miz-nan*
>The words **Los Angeles** becomes *liz-nos iz-nangeles*,
>because the *es* at the end of the word falls under Rule
>Numbers 6, 7, and 8
>The words **New York** becomes *niz-new yiz-nork*
>The word **paper** becomes *piz-na/piz-ner*
>The word **juice** becomes *jiz-nuice*

PARTITIVE NOUN

A partitive noun denotes a part of a whole. In English the words **some** or **any** are placed in front of the noun.

Example:
>The word **some** becomes *siz-nome*
>The word **any** becomes *iz-nany* because of the letter *a*,
>which is a vowel at beginning the word falling under Rule
>Number 5

PREPOSITIONS

Prepositions are short words that are usually in front of nouns that indicate location or relationship to the nouns.

Example:
>**above** becomes *iz-na/biz-nove*
>**about** becomes *iz-na/biz-nout*
>**across** becomes *iz-na/criz-noss*
>**after** becomes *iz-naf/tiz-ner*
>**ago** becomes *iz-na/giz-no*
>**at** becomes *iz-nat*

11

before becomes *biz-ne/fiz-nore*, pronounced *biz-nee/fiz-nor*

below becomes *biz-ne/liz-now*

besides becomes *biz-ne/siz-nides*

by becomes *biz-ny*

for becomes *fiz-nor*

from becomes *friz-nom*

in becomes *iz-nin*

into becomes *iz-nin/tiz-no*

near becomes *niz-near*

next to becomes *niz-next tiz-no*

off becomes *iz-noff*

on becomes *iz-non*

out of becomes *iz-nout iz-nof*

over becomes *iz-no/viz-ner*

past becomes *piz-nast*

to becomes *tiz-no*, which is pronounced *tiz-new*

towards becomes *tiz-no/wiz-nards*

through becomes *thriz-nough*

under becomes *iz-nunder*, which falls under Rule Number 6

until becomes *iz-nuntil*

ADJECTIVES

Adjectives describe nouns. Words such as tall, fat, dangerous are adjectives. Here are a few examples of how adjectives are used in sentences:

Example:

He is angry becomes *hiz-ne iz-nis iz-nan/griz-ny*

The dog was big becomes *thiz-ne diz-nog wiz-nas biz-nig*

I heard a Spanish man becomes *iz-ni hiz-neard iz-na spiz-nanish miz-nan*

POSSESSIVE ADJECTIVES

Possessive adjectives are words to show possession or ownership of something.

Example:
>   **my** becomes *miz-ny*
>   **your** becomes *yiz-nour*
>   **his** becomes *hiz-nis*
>   **her** becomes *hiz-ner*
>   **its** becomes *iz-nits*
>   **our** becomes *iz-nour*
>   **your** becomes *yiz-nour*
>   **their** becomes *thiz-neir*

DEFINITE ARTICLE

The purpose of a definite article is to introduce a noun. The only definite article in the English language is the word **the**. In spiz-neak the word **the** becomes *thiz-ne*, which would be pronounced *thiz-nuh*; exactly like it would sound in English if the word was not divided into half. Splitting any English word to convert it into spiz-neak never changes any of the original sounds.

INDEFINITE ARTICLE

The indefinite article is used to refer to something. In English there are only two indefinite articles, and they are **a** and **an**. For these two indefinite articles the sound *iz* stands alone with the letter *n* placed in front of these two words.

Example:
>   The word **a** becomes *iz-na*, and is pronounced *iz-nay*
>   The word **an** becomes *iz-nan*

VERB

A verb is a word that shows action, feeling, or state of being.

Example:
> The word **run** becomes *riz-nun*
> The word **love** becomes *liz-nove*
> The word **am** becomes *iz-nam*

CONJUGATED VERB

To conjugate a verb means to use the root word, but make a modification to it so that it will communicate when the action is taking place. When exactly the action takes place is called the verb tense. Although there are many tenses in English spiz-neak uses only Present Simple, Past Simple, and Future.

TO BE (tiz-no biz-ne), which is pronounced *tiz-noo biz-nee*

Present Simple

I am	*iz-ni iz-nam*	we are	*wiz-ne iz-nare*
you are	*yiz-nou iz-nare*	you are	*yiz-nou iz-are*
he is	*hiz-ne iz-nis*	they are	*thiz-ney iz-are*
she is	*shiz-ne iz-nis*		

Past Simple

I was	*iz-ni wiz-nas*	we were	*wiz-ne wiz-nere*
you were	*yiz-nou wiz-nere*	you were	*yiz-nou wiz-nere*
he was	*hiz-ne wiz-nas*	they were	*thiz-ney wiz-nere*
she was	*shiz-ne wiz-nas*		

To make English regular verbs past tense, that is to say past participles, the letters **ed** are placed at the end of the verb. The past participle of the verb **to push** is **pushed**, and to change this word into spiz-neak it becomes *piz-nushed*. The *ed* will always remain with the last syllable of a word.

Example:

The verb **to help** becomes *hiz-nelped*
The verb **to fill** becomes *fiz-nilled*
The verb **to escape** becomes *iz-nes|ciz-naped*

There are no rules for irregular verbs, and it is just a matter of practice.

Example:

The verb **bend** becomes **bent**, which becomes *biz-nent*
The verb **draw** becomes **drew**, which becomes *driz-new*
The verb **feel** becomes **felt**, which becomes *fiz-nelt*

Future

I will be	*iz-ni wiz-nill biz-ne*	we will be	*wiz-ne wiz-nill biz-ne*
you will be	*yiz-nou wiz-nill biz-ne*	you will be	*yiz-nou wiz-nill biz-ne*
he will be	*hiz-ne wiz-nill biz-ne*	they will be	*thiz-ney wiz-nill biz-ne*
she will be	*shiz-ne wiz-nill biz-ne*		

Again, tense are kept simple so that speaking is easier. Image how long and complicated it would be if you were to use the conditional tense of to be. It would look like this:

Conditional Perfect

I would have been becomes *iz-ni wiz-nould hiz-nave biz-neen*

The listener would need to be pay close attention to understand the meaning of the sentence. When people learn a foreign language they learn the simple forms of present, past, and future. Only after mastering them do they try conditional, subjunctive, and indicative tenses.

ADVERB

Adverbs give more information about a verb, and most are placed after a verb. The information given is usually how, how often, when, or when something was done.

Example:

> **He drove fast.** In spiz-neak it would be ***hiz-ne driz-nove fiz-nast***, and ***fiz-nast*** is the adverb
>
> **You speak too slow** would be ***yiz-nou spiz-neak tiz-noo sliz-now.*** The word ***tiz-noo*** is the adverb
>
> **She is very persistent** would be ***shiz-ne iz-nis viz-nery piz-ner/siz-nis/tiz-nent***. The word ***piz-ner/siz-nis/tiz-nent*** is the adverb

DEMONSTRATIVES

Demonstratives indicate where a person, object, or an event is in relation to the speaker. Here is a list of them:

Example:

> **This** becomes ***thiz-nis***
> **That** becomes ***thiz-nat***
> **These** becomes ***thiz-nese***
> **Those** becomes ***thiz-nose***

Here are a few sentences using demonstratives:

Example:

> **Is this the hotel?** becomes ***iz-nis thiz-nis thiz-ne hiz-no/tiz-nel?***
>
> **That is my book you took!** becomes ***thiz-nat iz-nis miz-ny biz-nook yiz-nou tiz-nook!***

16

These are my sisters becomes *thiz-nese iz-nare miz-ny siz-nis|tiz-ners*

Those clothes don't fit becomes *thiz-nose cliz-nothes diz-non't fiz-nit*

NUMBERS (niz-num|biz-ners)

Cardinal numbers: 1 to 1000

0 **zero** becomes *ziz-nero*
1 **one** becomes *iz-none*
2 **two** becomes *twiz-no*, the *no* is pronounced *oo* as in *boot*
3 **three** becomes *thriz-nee*
4 **four** becomes *fiz-nour*
5 **five** becomes *fiz-nive*
6 **six** becomes *siz-nix*
7 **seven** become *siz-ne|viz-nen*
8 **eight** becomes *iz-neight*
9 **nine** becomes *niz-nine*
10 **ten** becomes *tiz-nen*
11 **eleven** becomes *iz-ne|liz-neven*, see Rule Number 7
12 **twelve** becomes *twiz-nelve*
13 **thirteen** becomes *thiz-nir|tiz-neen*
14 **fourteen** becomes *fiz-nour|tiz-neen*
15 **fifteen** becomes *fiz-nif|tiz-neen*
16 **sixteen** become *siz-nix|tiz-neen*
17 **seventeen** becomes *siz-nev|en|tiz-neen*, see Rule Number 3
18 **eighteen** becomes *iz-neigh|tiz-neen*
19 **nineteen** becomes *niz-nine|tiz-neen*
20 **twenty** becomes *twiz-nen|tiz-ny*
21 **twenty-one** becomes *twiz-nen|tiz-ny iz-none*
22 **twenty-two** becomes *twiz-nen|tiz-ny twiz-no*
30 **thirty** becomes *thiz-nir|tiz-ny*
31 **thirty-one** becomes *thiz-nir|tiz-ny iz-none*
32 **thirty-two** becomes *thiz-nir|tiz-ny twiz-no*
40 **forty** becomes *fiz-nor|tiz-ny*

41 **forty-one** becomes *fiz-nor/tiz-ny iz-none*
42 **forty-two** becomes *fiz-nor/tiz-ny twiz-no*
50 **fifty** becomes *fiz-nif/tiz-ny*
51 **fifty-one** becomes *fiz-nif/tiz-ny iz-none*
52 **fifty-two** becomes *fiz-nif/tiz-ny twiz-no*
60 **sixty** becomes *siz-nix/tiz-ny*
61 **sixty-one** becomes *siz-nix/tiz-ny iz-none*
62 **sixty-two** becomes *siz-nix/tiz-ny twiz-no*
70 **seventy** becomes *siz-nev/en/tiz-ny*
71 **seventy-one** becomes *siz-nev/en/tiz-ny iz-none*
72 **seventy-two** becomes *siz-nev/en/tiz-ny twiz-no*
80 **eighty** becomes *iz-neigh/tiz-ny*
81 **eighty-one** becomes *iz-neigh/tiz-ny iz-none*
82 **eighty-two** becomes *iz-neigh/tiz-ny twiz-no*
90 **ninety** becomes *niz-nine/tiz-ny*
91 **ninety-one** becomes *niz-nine/tiz-ny iz-none*
92 **ninety-two** becomes *niz-nine/tiz-ny twiz-no*

Past tense verbs that end with the letters **ed** will always remain with the last syllable of a word. However, numbers are not verbs, and this rule does not apply to numbers.

100 **one hundred** becomes *iz-none hiz-nun/driz-ned*
101 **one hundred one** becomes *iz-none hiz-nun/driz-ned iz-none*
102 **one hundred two** becomes *iz-none hiz-nun/driz-ned twiz-no*
200 **two hundred** becomes *twiz-no hiz-nun/driz-ned*
201 **two hundred one** becomes *twiz-no hiz-nun/driz-ned iz-none*
202 **two hundred two** becomes *twiz-no hiz-nun/driz-ed twiz-no*
300 **three hundred** becomes *thriz-nee hiz-nun/driz-ned*
301 **three hundred one** becomes *thriz-nee hiz-nun/driz-ned iz-none*
302 **three hundred two** becomes *thiz-nee hiz-nun/driz-ned twiz-no*
400 **four hundred** becomes *fiz-nour hiz-nun/driz-ned*
401 **four hundred one** becomes *fiz-nour hiz-nun/driz-ned iz-none*
402 **four hundred two** becomes *fiz-nour hiz-nun/driz-ned twiz-no*
500 **five hundred** becomes *fiz-nive hiz-nun/driz-ned*
501 **five hundred one** becomes *fiz-nive hiz-nun/driz-ned iz-one*
502 **five hundred two** becomes *fiz-nive hiz-nun/driz-ned twiz-no*
600 **six hundred** becomes *siz-nix hiz-nun/driz-ned*

601 **six hundred one** becomes *siz-nix hiz-nun|driz-ned iz-none*
602 **six hundred two** becomes *siz-nix hiz-nun|driz-ned twiz-no*
700 **seven hundred** becomes *siz-ne|viz-nen hiz-nun|driz-ned*
701 **seven hundred one** becomes *siz-ne|viz-nen hiz-nun|driz-ned iz-none*
702 **seven hundred two** becomes *siz-ne|viz-nen hiz-nun|driz-ned twiz-no*
800 **eight hundred** becomes *iz-neight hiz-nun|driz-ned*
801 **eight hundred one** becomes *iz-neight hiz-nun|driz-ned iz-one*
802 **eight hundred two** becomes *iz-neight hiz-nun|driz-ned twiz-no*
900 **nine hundred** becomes *niz-nine hiz-nun|driz-ned*
901 **nine hundred one** becomes *niz-nine hiz-nun|driz-ned iz-none*
902 **nine hundred two** becomes *niz-nine hiz-nun|driz-ned twiz-no*
1000 **one thousand** becomes *iz-none thiz-nou|siz-nand*
1001 **one thousand one** becomes *iz-none thiz-nou|siz-nand iz-none*
1002 **one thousand two** becomes *iz-none thiz-nou|siz-nand twiz-no*

ORDINAL NUMBERS (iz-nor|diz-ninal niz-num|biz-ners)

First to Twentieth:

1st **First** becomes *fiz-nirst*
2nd **Second** becomes *siz-ne|ciz-nond*
3rd **Third** becomes *thiz-nird*
4th **Fourth** becomes *fiz-nourth*
5th **Fifth** becomes *fiz-nifth*
6th **Sixth** becomes *siz-nixth*
7th **Seventh** becomes *siz-ne|viz-nenth*
8th **Eighth** becomes *iz-neighth*
9th **Ninth** becomes *niz-ninth*

10th **Tenth** becomes *tiz-nenth*
11th **Eleventh** becomes *iz-ne/liz-ne/viz-nenth*
12th **Twelfth** becomes *twiz-nelfth*
13th **Thirteenth** becomes *thiz-nir/tiz-neenth*
14th **Fourteenth** becomes *fiz-nour/tiz-neenth*
15th **Fifteenth** becomes *fiz-nif/tiz-neenth*
16th **Sixteenth** becomes *siz-nix/tiz-neenth*
17th **Seventeenth** becomes *siz-nev/en/tiz-neenth*
18th **Eighteenth** becomes *iz-neigh/tiz-neenth*
19th **Nineteenth** becomes *niz-nine/tiz-neenth*
20th **Twentieth** becomes *twiz-nen/tiz-nieth*

DAYS (diz-nays)

The days of the week:

Sunday becomes *siz-nun/diz-nay*
Monday becomes *mis-nun/diz-nay*
Tuesday becomes *tiz-nues/diz-nay*
Wednesday becomes *wiz-nednes/diz-nay*
Thursday becomes *thiz-nurs/diz-nay*
Friday becomes *friz-ni/diz-nay*
Saturday becomes *siz-nat/ur/diz-nay*

MONTHS (miz-nonths)

The months of the year:

January becomes *jiz-nan/u/iz-nary*
February becomes *fiz-neb/riz-nu/iz-ary*
March becomes *miz-narch*
April becomes *iz-nap/riz-nil*
May becomes *miz-nay*
June becomes *jiz-nune*
July becomes *jiz-nu/liz-ny*, and the letter **y** is pronounce like **i**
August becomes *iz-nau|giz-nust*
September becomes *siz-nep/tiz-nem/biz-ner*

October becomes *iz-noc/tiz-no/biz-ner*
November becomes *niz-nov/viz-nem/biz-ner*
December becomes *diz-ne/ciz-nem/biz-ner*

CARDINAL DIRECTIONS (ciz-nard|i|niz-nal diz-ni|riz-nections)

north becomes *niz-north*
south becomes *siz-nouth*
east becomes *iz-neast*
west becomes *wiz-nest*

SEASONS (siz-nea|siz-nons)

The seasons of the year:

Spring becomes *spr-iz/ning*, Rule Number 7 does not apply to this word because it is only one syllable
Summer becomes *siz-num/miz-ner*
Fall becomes *fiz-nall*
Winter becomes *wiz-nin/tiz-ner*

TELLING TIME (tiz-nelling tiz-nime)

Time expressions:

What time is it? becomes *whiz-nat tiz-nime iz-nis iz-nit?*
It is noon becomes *iz-nit iz-nis niz-noon*
It is one o'clock becomes *iz-nit iz-nis iz-none iz-no/cliz-nock*
It is one fifteen becomes *iz-nit iz-nis iz-none fiz-nif/tiz-neen*
It is two thirty becomes *iz-nit iz-nis twiz-no thiz-nir/tiz-ny*
At what time? becomes *iz-nat whiz-nat tiz-nime?*
At midnight becomes iz-*nat miz-nid/niz-night*
At three in the morning becomes *iz-nat thriz-nee iz-nin thiz-ne miz-norning*
In half an hour becomes *iz-nin hiz-nalf iz-nan hiz-nour*

In five minutes becomes *iz-nin fiz-nive miz-ni/niz-nutes*
Eight seconds left becomes *iz-neight siz-ne/ciz-nonds*

BASIC EXPRESSIONS (biz-na|siz-nic iz-nex-|priz-nessions)

Yes becomes *yiz-nes*
No becomes *niz-no*
Please becomes *pliz-nease*
Thank you becomes *thiz-nank yiz-nou*
Thanks becomes *thiz-nanks*
No thanks becomes *niz-no thiz-nanks*
Excuse me becomes *iz-nex/ciz-nuse miz-ne*
You're welcome becomes *yiz-nou're wiz-nel/ciz-nome*

GREETINGS (griz-neetings)

Good morning becomes *giz-nood miz-norning*
Good afternoon becomes *giz-nood iz-naf/tiz-ner/niz-noon*
Good evening becomes *giz-nood iz-nevening*
Good night becomes *giz-nood niz-night*
Good bye becomes *giz-nood biz-nye*
Bye becomes *biz-nye*
See you later becomes *siz-nee yiz-nou liz-nater*
See you tomorrow becomes *siz-nee yiz-nou tiz-no/miz-nor/riz-now*
Ciao (the Italian word for good bye) becomes *ciz-nao*

Hello becomes *hiz-nel/liz-no*
Hi becomes *hiz-ni*
How are you? becomes *hiz-now iz-nare yiz-nou?*
I am good, thanks becomes *iz-ni iz-nam giz-nood, thiz-nanks*
Nice to meet you becomes *niz-nice tiz-no miz-neet yiz-nou*
Fine becomes *fiz-nine*
I am bad becomes *iz-ni iz-nam biz-nad*

I am tired becomes *iz-ni iz-nam tiz-nired*, and remember the rule that *ed* at the end of a past tense verb will always remain with the last syllable of a word

I am sick becomes *iz-ni iz-nam siz-nick*
And you? becomes *iz-nand yiz-nou?*
Excuse me becomes *iz-nex|ciz-nuse miz-ne*

What is your name? becomes *whiz-nat iz-nis yiz-nour niz-name?*
My name is _____ becomes *miz-ny niz-name iz-nis _____*
Here is my phone number becomes *hiz-nere iz-nis miz-ny phiz-none niz-num|biz-ner*
Is she your friend? becomes *iz-nis shiz-ne yiz-nour friz-niend?*
I am hopeful becomes *iz-ni iz-nam hiz-nope|fiz-nul*
Text me becomes *tiz-next miz-ne*

QUESTIONS (quiz-nes|tions)

Where? becomes *whiz-nere?*
How? becomes *hiz-now?*
When? becomes *whiz-nen?*
What? becomes *whiz-nat?*
Why? becomes *whiz-ny?*
Who? becomes *whiz-no?*
Which? becomes *whiz-nich?*
Where is? becomes *whiz-nere iz-nis?*
Where are? becomes *whiz-nere iz-nare?*
How much? becomes *hiz-now miz-nuch?*
How many? becomes *hiz-now miz-nany?*
How far? becomes *hiz-now fiz-nar?*
How long? becomes **hiz-now liz-nong?**
How much does it cost? becomes *hiz-now miz-nuch diz-noes iz-nit ciz-nost?*
When does it open? becomes *whiz-nen diz-noes iz-nit iz-no|piz-nen?*
What do you call this? becomes *whiz-nat diz-no yiz-nou ciz-nall thiz-nis?*

What do you mean? becomes *whiz-nat diz-no yiz-nou miz-nean?*
Do you speak spiz-neak? becomes *diz-no yiz-nou spiz-neak spiz-neak?*
Could you speak slower? becomes *ciz-nould yiz-nou spiz-neak sliz-nower?*
Could you repeat that? becomes *ciz-nould yiz-nou riz-ne/piz-neat thiz-nat?*
I understand becomes *iz-ni iz-nunder/stiz-nand*
I don't understand becomes *iz-ni diz-non't iz-nunder/stiz-nand*
Can I have? becomes *ciz-nan iz-ni hiz-nave?*
Can we have? becomes *ciz-nan wiz-ne hiz-nave?*
Can you show me? becomes *ciz-nan yiz-nou shiz-now miz-ne?*
I can't become *iz-ni ciz-nan't*
Can you tell me? becomes *ciz-nan yiz-nou tiz-nell miz-ne?*
Where is your locker? becomes *whiz-nere iz-nis yiz-nour liz-noc/kiz-ner?*

WANTING (wiz-nanting)

I'd like become *iz-ni'ed liz-nike*
We'd like becomes *wiz-ne'd liz-nike*
What do you want? becomes *whiz-nat diz-no yiz-nou wiz-nant?*
Give me becomes *giz-nive miz-ne*
Give it to me becomes *giz-nive iz-nit tiz-no miz-ne*
Bring me becomes *briz-ning miz-ne*
Bring it to me becomes *briz-ning iz-nit tiz-no miz-ne*
Show me becomes *shiz-now miz-ne*
Show it to me becomes *shiz-now iz-nit tiz-no miz-ne*
I'm looking for becomes *iz-ni'm liz-nooking fiz-nor*
I'm hungry becomes *iz-ni'm hiz-nun/griz-ny*
I'm thirsty becomes *iz-ni'm thiz-nir/stiz-ny*
I'm tired becomes *iz-ni'm tiz-nired*
It's important becomes *iz-nit's iz-nimport/tiz-nant*
It's urgent! becomes *iz-nit's iz-nur/giz-nent!*
Hurry up! becomes *hiz-nur/riz-ny iz-nup!*

OPPOSITES (iz-nop|piz-no|siz-nites)

big/small becomes *biz-nig/smiz-nall*
clean/dirty becomes *cliz-nean/diz-nir|tiz-ny*
quick/slow becomes *quiz-nick/sliz-now*
hot/cold becomes *hiz-not/ciz-nold*
cool/warm becomes *ciz-nool/wiz-narm*
full/empty becomes *fiz-null/iz-nemp|tiz-ny*
easy/difficult becomes *iz-nea|siz-ny/diz-nif|fiz-ni|ciz-nult*
hard/soft becomes *hiz-nard/siz-noft*
heavy/light becomes *hiz-ne|viz-ny/liz-night*
light/dark becomes *liz-night/diz-nark*
open/shut becomes *iz-nopen/shiz-nut*, see Rule Number 7
right/wrong becomes *riz-night/wriz-nong*
old/new becomes *iz-nold/niz-new*
old/young becomes *iz-nold/yiz-noung*
beautiful/ugly becomes *biz-nea|u|tiz-niful/iz-nug|liz-ny*
free (vacant)/occupied becomes *friz-nee/iz-nocc|u|piz-nied*
good/bad becomes *giz-nood/biz-nad*
good/evil becomes *giz-nood/iz-nevil*
better/worse becomes *biz-net|tiz-ner/wiz-norse*
here/there becomes *hiz-nere/thiz-nere*
early/late becomes *iz-nearl|liz-ny/liz-nate*
cheap/expensive becomes *chiz-neap/iz-nexpen|siz-nive*
near/far becomes *niz-near/fiz-nar*
first/last becomes *fiz-nirst/liz-nast*
rich/poor becomes *riz-nich/piz-noor*
smooth/rough becomes *smiz-nooth/riz-nough*
true/false becomes *triz-nue/fiz-nalse*
happy/sad becomes *hiz-nap|piz-ny/siz-nad*
enter/exit becomes *iz-nenter/iz-nexit*
work/relax becomes *wiz-nork/riz-ne|liz-nax*

QUANTITIES (quiz-nant|i|tiz-nies)

a little/a lot becomes *iz-na liz-nittle/iz-na liz-not*
few/a few becomes *fiz-new/iz-na fiz-new*
much becomes *miz-nuch*

many becomes *miz-nany*
more/less becomes *miz-nore/liz-ness*
more than/less than becomes *miz-nore thiz-nan/liz-ness thiz-nan*
enough/too much becomes *iz-nenough/tiz-noo miz-nuch*
some/any becomes *siz-nome/iz-nany*

DIRECTIONS (diz-ri|riz-nections)

Please, turn there at the corner becomes *pliz-nease, tiz-nurn thiz-nere iz-nat thiz-ne ciz-nor|niz-ner*

Continue to the stop light becomes *ciz-non|tiz-ninue tiz-no thiz-ne stiz-nop liz-night*

How far is it? becomes *hiz-now fiz-nar iz-nis iz-nit?*

It is close becomes *iz-nit iz-nis cliz-nose*

It is far becomes *iz-nit iz-nis fiz-nar*

Stop here becomes *stiz-nop hiz-nere*

Straight ahead becomes *striz-naight iz-na|hiz-nead*

Turn left becomes *tiz-nurn liz-neft*

Turn right becomes *tiz-nurn riz-night*

Where is the train station? becomes *whiz-nere iz-nis thiz-ne triz-nain stiz-nation?*

I can't. We are going to the airport today becomes *iz-ni ciz-nan't. wiz-ne iz-nare giz-noing tiz-no thiz-ne iz-nair|piz-nort tiz-no|diz-nay*

At the corner becomes *iz-nat thiz-ne ciz-nor|niz-ner*

At the light becomes *iz-nat thiz-ne liz-night*

That way becomes *thiz-nat wiz-nay*

Two blocks ahead becomes *twiz-no bliz-nocks iz-na|hiz-nead*

U-turn becomes *iz-nu|tiz-nurn*

Five miles becomes *fiz-nive miz-niles*

Six meters becomes *siz-nix miz-ne|tiz-ners*

Three kilometers becomes *thriz-nee kiz-nil|o|miz-ne|tiz-ners*

One kilo becomes **iz-none kiz-nilo**

It is a very bad road becomes *iz-nit iz-nis iz-na viz-ne|riz-ny biz-nad riz-noad*

DISTRESS (diz-ni|striz-ness)

Be careful becomes *biz-ne ciz-nare|fiz-nul*

Help! becomes *hiz-nelp!*

Call the police! becomes *ciz-nall thiz-ne piz-no|liz-nice!*

That man is crazy! becomes *thiz-nat miz-nan iz-nis criz-na|ziz-ny!*

I am afraid of him! becomes *iz-ni iz-nam iz-na|friz-naid iz-nof hiz-nim!*

Don't tell her! becomes *diz-non't tiz-nell hiz-ner!*

He has a gun becomes *hiz-ne hiz-nas iz-na giz-nun*

She carries a knife becomes *shiz-ne ciz-nar/riz-nies iz-na kniz-nife*

Don't go with him! becomes *diz-no'nt giz-no wiz-nith hiz-nim!*

COLORS (ciz-no|liz-nors)

beige becomes *biz-neige*
black becomes *bliz-nack*
blue becomes *bliz-nue*
brown becomes *briz-nown*
cyan becomes *ciz-nyan*
gold becomes *giz-nold*
gray becomes *griz-nay*
green becomes *griz-neen*
ivory becomes *iz-ni/viz-ory*
lavender becomes *liz-nav/en/diz-ner*
magenta becomes *miz-na/giz-nenta*
maroon becomes *miz-na/riz-noon*
navy becomes *niz-na/viz-ny*
orange becomes *iz-norange*
pink becomes *piz-nink*
purple becomes *piz-nurple*
red becomes *riz-ned*
salmon becomes *siz-nal/miz-non*
tan becomes *tiz-nan*
white becomes *whiz-nite*
yellow becomes *yiz-nel/liz-now*

FAMILY (fiz-nam|i|liz-ny)

relatives becomes *riz-nel/a/tiz-nives*
father becomes *fiz-na/thiz-ner*
dad becomes *diz-nad*
mother becomes *miz-no/thiz-ner*
mom becomes *miz-nom*
parents becomes *piz-na/riz-nents*

grandfather becomes *griz-nand|friz-na|thiz-ner*
grandpa becomes *griz-nand|piz-na*
grandmother becomes *griz-nand|miz-no|thiz-ner*
grandma becomes *griz-nand|miz-na*
child becomes *chiz-nild*
children becomes *chiz-nild|riz-nen*
brother becomes *briz-no|thiz-ner*
bro becomes *briz-no*
sister becomes *siz-nis|tiz-ner*
sis becomes *siz-nis*
son becomes *siz-non*
daughter becomes *diz-naugh|tiz-ner*
uncle becomes *iz-nuncle*
aunt becomes *iz-naunt*
cousin becomes *ciz-nou|siz-nin*
in-laws becomes *iz-nin|liz-naws*
step brother becomes *stiz-nep briz-no|thiz-ner*

I have a sister becomes *iz-ni hiz-nave iz-na siz-nis|tiz-ner*

We have two cousins becomes *wiz-ne hiz-nave twiz-no ciz-nou|siz-nins*

I don't have a brother becomes *iz-ni diz-non't hiz-nave iz-na briz-no|thiz-ner*

This is my family becomes *thiz-nis iz-nis mis-ny fiz-nam|i|liz-ny*

Is that your mother? becomes *iz-nis thiz-nat yiz-nour miz-no|thiz-ner?*

HOME (hiz-nome)

attic becomes *iz-nat|tiz-nic*
backyard becomes *biz-nack|yiz-nard*
balcony becomes *biz-nal|ciz-no|niz-ny*
basement becomes *biz-nase|miz-nent*

bath becomes *biz-nath*
bathroom becomes *biz-nath/riz-noom*
bathtub becomes *biz-nath/tiz-nub*
bed becomes *biz-ned*
bedroom becomes *bez-ned/riz-noom*
bidet becomes *biz-ni/diz-net*
ceiling becomes *ciz-nei/liz-ning*
chair becomes *chiz-nair*
chimney becomes *chiz-nim/niz-ney*
closet becomes *cliz-no/siz-net*
couch becomes *ciz-nouch*
dining room becomes *diz-ning riz-noom*
dishes becomes *diz-nishes*
dishwasher becomes *diz-nish/wiz-nasher*
door becomes *diz-noor*
dresser becomes *driz-nes/siz-ner*
driveway becomes *driz-nive/wiz-nay*
fence becomes *fiz-nence*
fireplace becomes *fiz-nire/pliz-nace*
floor becomes *fliz-noor*
flower becomes *fliz-nower*
garage becomes *giz-na/riz-nage*
garden becomes *giz-narden*
garden hose becomes *giz-narden hiz-nose*
grass becomes *griz-nass*
hallway becomes *hiz-nall/wiz-nay*
hot tub becomes *hiz-not tiz-nub*
house becomes *hiz-nouse*
kitchen becomes *kiz-nit/chiz-nen*
laundry room becomes *liz-naun/driz-ny riz-noom*
lawn becomes *liz-nawn*
living room becomes *liz-niving riz-noom*
mailbox becomes *miz-nail/biz-nox*
microwave becomes *miz-ni/criz-no/wiz-nave*
office becomes *iz-nof/fiz-nice*
oven becomes *iz-noven*
patio becomes *piz-na/tiz-nio*
pet becomes *piz-net*

pillow becomes *piz-nil/liz-now*
pool becomes *piz-nool*
refrigerator becomes *riz-ne/friz-nig/e/riz-nator*
roof becomes *riz-noof*
room becomes *riz-noom*
rug becomes *riz-nug*
sheet becomes *shiz-neet*
shower becomes *shiz-nower*
sidewalk becomes *siz-nide/wiz-nalk*
sink becomes *siz-nink*
sofa becomes *siz-no/fiz-na*
stairs becomes *stiz-nairs*
stove becomes *stiz-nove*
toilet becomes *tiz-noi/liz-net*
trash becomes *triz-nash*
tree becomes *triz-nee*
wall becomes *wiz-nall*
window becomes *wiz-nin/diz-now*

FOOD (fiz-nood)

apple becomes *iz-napple*
apricot becomes *iz-nap/riz-ni/ciz-not*
artichoke becomes *iz-nart/i/chiz-noke*
asparagus becomes *iz-na/spiz-nar/a/giz-nus*
avocado becomes *iz-nav/o/ciz-nado*
bacon becomes *biz-na/ciz-non*
bagel becomes *biz-na/giz-nel*
banana becomes **biz-na|niz-nana**
beans becomes *biz-neans*
beef becomes *biz-neef*
bread becomes *briz-nead*
broccoli becomes *briz-noc/ciz-noli*
brownie becomes *briz-now/niz-nie*
brussels sprouts becomes *briz-nus/siz-nels spriz-nouts*
burrito becomes *biz-nur/riz-nito*
butter becomes *biz-nut/tiz-ner*

cabbage becomes *ciz-nab/biz-nage*
cake becomes *ciz-nake*
cauliflower becomes *ciz-naul/i/fliz-nower*
cereal becomes *ciz-ne/riz-neal*
carrots becomes *ciz-nar/riz-nots*
cheese becomes *chiz-neese*
cherry becomes *chiz-nerry*
chicken becomes *chiz-nic/kiz-nen*
chilli becomes *chiz-nil/liz-ni*
chips becomes *chiz-nips*
chocolate becomes *chiz-noc/o/liz-nate*
cinnamon becomes *ciz-nin/niz-na/miz-non*
clams becomes *cliz-nams*
cod becomes *ciz-nod*
coke becomes *ciz-noke*
cola becomes *ciz-nola*
cold cuts becomes *ciz-nold ciz-nuts*
cookie becomes *ciz-noo/kiz-ne*
corn becomes *ciz-norn*
cotton candy becomes *ciz-not/tiz-non ciz-nan/diz-ny*
cream becomes *criz-neam*
croissant becomes *criz-noi/ssiz-nant*
dates becomes *diz-nates*
dessert becomes *diz-nes/siz-nert*
dip becomes *diz-nip*
donut becomes *diz-no/niz-nut*
dough becomes *diz-nough*
drive-thru becomes *driz-nive thriz-nu*
ginger becomes *giz-nin/giz-ner*
duck becomes *diz-nuck*
egg becomes *iz-negg*
eggnog becomes *iz-negg/niz-nog*
English muffin becomes *iz-nenglish miz-nuf/fiz-in*
fig becomes *fiz-nig*
fish becomes *fiz-nish*, which is an exception to Rule Number 7
flour becomes *fliz-nour*
French fries becomes *friz-nench friz-nies*
French toast becomes *friz-nech tiz-noast*

fresh becomes *friz-nesh*
fruit becomes *friz-nuit*
garlic becomes *giz-nar|liz-nic*
grape becomes *griz-nape*
green bean becomes *griz-neen biz-nean*
grits becomes *griz-nits*
guacamole becomes *guiz-nac|a|miz-nole*
ham becomes *hiz-nam*
hamburger becomes *hiz-nam|biz-nur|giz-ner*
herbs becomes *hiz-nerbs or iz-n'herbs*
honey becomes *hiz-no|niz-ney*
hotdog becomes *hiz-not|diz-nog*
hot sauce becomes *hiz-not siz-nauce*
ice cream becomes *iz-nice criz-neam*
jam becomes *jiz-nam*
jelly becomes *jiz-nel|liz-ny*
ketchup becomes *kiz-net|chiz-nup*
kiwi becomes *kiz-ni|wiz-ni*
lemon becomes *liz-ne|miz-non*
lettuce becomes *liz-net|tiz-nuce*
liqourice becomes *liz-niq|ou|riz-nice*
liver becomes *liz-niver*
lobster becomes *liz-nob|stiz-ner*
marmalade becomes *miz-nar|miz-na|liz-nade*
mayonnaise becomes *miz-nay|o|nniz-naise*
meat becomes *miz-neat*
medium well becomes *miz-ne|diz-nium wiz-nell*
melon becomes *miz-nelon*
menu becomes *miz-nenu*
milk becomes *miz-nilk*
mint becomes *miz-nint*
mocha becomes *miz-nocha*
mushroom becomes *miz-nush|riz-noom*
mussels becomes *miz-nussels*
mustard becomes *miz-nus|tiz-nard*
nectarine becomes *niz-nec|tiz-na|riz-nine*
noodles becomes *niz-noodles*
nut becomes *niz-nut*

oatmeal becomes *iz-noat/miz-neal*
oil becomes *iz-noil*
olives becomes *iz-nolives*, the *es* ending follows Rule Number 7
omlette becomes *iz-nom/liz-nette*
onion becomes *iz-nonion*, the *ion* ending follows Rule Number 7
onion rings becomes *iz-nonion riz-nings*
pasta becomes *piz-na/stiz-na*
peanut becomes *piz-nea/niz-nut*
peanut butter becomes *piz-nea/niz-nut biz-nut/tiz-ner*
peach becomes *piz-neach*
pear becomes *piz-near*
peas becomes *piz-neas*
pepper becomes *piz-nep/piz-ner*
pickle becomes *piz-nickle*
pineapple becomes *piz-nine/iz-napple*
pizza becomes *piz-niz/ziz-na*
plum becomes *pliz-num*
popcorn becomes *piz-nop/ciz-norn*
potato becomes *piz-no/tiz-nato*
pork becomes *piz-nork*
poultry becomes *piz-noul/triz-ny*
prawns becomes *priz-nawns*
pumpkin becomes *piz-nump/kiz-nin*
radish becomes *riz-na/diz-nish*
raisin becomes *riz-nai/siz-nin*
raspberry becomes *riz-nasp/biz-ner/riz-ny*
relish becomes *riz-nelish*
rabbit becomes *riz-nab/biz-nit*
rare becomes *riz-nare*
raw becomes *riz-naw*
rice becomes *riz-nice*
roll becomes *riz-noll*
salad becomes *siz-nalad*
salami becomes *siz-na/liz-na/miz-ni*
salmon becomes *siz-nal/miz-non*
salt becomes *siz-nalt*
sauce becomes *siz-nauce*
sauerkraut becomes *siz-nau/er/kriz-naut*

sausage becomes *siz-nau|siz-nage*
seafood becomes *siz-nea|fiz-nood*
seasoning becomes *siz-nea|siz-noning*
shrimp becomes *shriz-nimp*
snow cone becomes *sniz-now ciz-none*
spegehetti becomes *spiz-ne|giz-nehet|tiz-ni*
spicy becomes *spiz-ni|ciz-ny*
spinach becomes *spiz-ninach*
sprouts becomes *spriz-nouts*
soup becomes *siz-noup*
sour becomes *siz-nour*
soy becomes *siz-noy*
squash becomes *squiz-nuash*
steak becomes *stiz-neak*
steak sauce becomes *stiz-neak siz-nauce*
stew becomes *stiz-new*
strawberry becomes *striz-naw|biz-ner|riz-ny*
sugar becomes *siz-nu|giz-nar*
sushi becomes *siz-nu|shiz-ni*
sweet becomes *swiz-neet*
sweet potatoes becomes *swiz-neet piz-no|tiz-natoes*
swordfish becomes *swiz-nord|fiz-nish*
syrup becomes *siz-nyrup*
taco becomes *tiz-na|ciz-no*
toast becomes *tiz-noast*
tomato becomes *tiz-mo|miz-nato*
turkey becomes *tiz-nur|kiz-ney*
turnip becomes *tiz-nur|niz-nip*
vegetable becomes *viz-neg|e|tiz-able*
vegetarian becomes *viz-neg|e|tiz-narian*
vanilla becomes *viz-na|niz-nil|liz-na*
vinegar becomes *viz-nin|e|giz-nar*
waffle becomes *wiz-naffle*
wasabi becomes *wiz-na|siz-nabi*
watermelon becomes *wiz-na|tiz-ner|miz-nelon*
well done becomes *wiz-nell diz-none*
yam becomes *yiz-nam*
zucchini becomes *ziz-nu|cchini*

DRINK (driz-nink)

apple juice becomes *iz-napple jiz-nuice*
coffee becomes *ciz-nof|fiz-nee*
coke becomes *ciz-noke*
cranberry juice becomes *criz-nan|biz-ner|riz-ny jiz-nuice*
energy drink becomes *iz-en|er|giz-ney*
grapefruit juice becomes *griz-nape|friz-nuit jiz-nuice*
grape juice becomes *griz-nape jiz-nuice*
hot chocolate becomes *hiz-not chiz-noc|o|liz-nate*
lemonade becomes *liz-nem|o|niz-nade*
milk becomes *miz-nilk*
milkshake becomes *miz-nilk|shiz-nake*
orange juice becomes *iz-norange jiz-nuice*
pineapple juice becomes *piz-nine|iz-napple jiz-nuice*
protein drink becomes *priz-no|tiz-nein driz-nink*
shake becomes *shiz-nake*
straw becomes *striz-naw*
tea becomes *tiz-nea*
tomato juice becomes *tiz-mo|miz-nato jiz-nuice*
water becomes *wiz-na|tiz-ner*

PLACE SETTING (pliz-nace siz-net|tiz-ning)

bowl becomes *biz-nowl*
bread plate becomes *briz-nead pliz-nate*
butter dish becomes *biz-nut|tiz-ner diz-nish*
butter knife becomes *biz-nut|tiz-ner kniz-nife*
cup becomes *ciz-nup*
dessert spoon becomes *diz-nes|siz-nert spiz-noon*
dinner fork becomes *diz-nin|niz-ner fiz-nork*
fork become *fiz-nork*
glass becomes *gliz-nass*
knife becomes *kniz-nife*
menu becomes *miz-nenu*
napkin becomes *niz-nap|kiz-nin*
napkin ring becomes *niz-nap|kiz-nin riz-ning*

pepper mill becomes *piz-nep/piz-ner miz-nill*
pepper shaker *piz-nep/piz-ner shiz-naker*
pitcher becomes *piz-nit/chiz-ner*
placecard becomes *piz-nace/ciz-nard*
place mat becomes *pliz-nace miz-nat*
plate becomes *pliz-nate*
salad fork becomes *siz-nalad fiz-nork*
salad plate becomes *siz-nalad pliz-nate*
salt shaker becomes *siz-nalt shiz-naker*
saucer becomes *siz-nau/ciz-ner*
spoon becomes *spiz-noon*
soup spoon becomes *siz-noup spiz-noon*
tablecloth becomes *tiz-nable/cliz-noth*
teaspoon becomes *tiz-nea/spiz-noon*
water goblet becomes *wiz-na/tiz-ner giz-nob/liz-net*

CLOTHES (cliz-nothes)

baseball hat becomes *biz-nase/biz-nall hiz-nat*
belt becomes *biz-nelt*
blouse becomes *bliz-nouse*
boot becomes *biz-noot*
bra becomes *briz-na*
button becomes *biz-nut/tiz-non*
cap becomes *ciz-nap*
coat becomes *ciz-noat*
dress becomes *driz-ness*
glove becomes *gliz-nove*
hat becomes *hiz-nat*
high heel becomes *hiz-nigh hiz-neel*
hoodie becomes *hiz-noodie*
pants becomes *piz-nants*
robe becomes *riz-nobe*
sandle becomes *siz-nandle*
scarf becomes *sciz-narf*
shoe becomes *shiz-noe*
shorts becomes *shiz-norts*

skirt becomes *skiz-nirt*
slipper becomes *sliz-nip|piz-ner*
sock becomes *siz-nock*
stocking becomes *stiz-nocking*
suit becomes *siz-nuit*
sweater becomes *swiz-nea|tiz-ner*
tie becomes *tiz-nie*
underwear becomes *iz-nunder|wiz-near*
vest becomes *viz-nest*

CLOTHING ACCESSORIES (cliz-nothing iz-nac|ciz-nes|niz-ories)

blush becomes *bliz-nush*
bracelet becomes *briz-nace|liz-net*
earring becomes *iz-near|riz-ning*
glasses becomes *gliz-nas|siz-nes*
headband becomes *hiz-nead|biz-nand*
mascara becomes *miz-na|sciz-na|riz-na*
nail polish becomes *niz-nail piz-nolish*, due to Rule Number 7
necklace becomes *niz-neck|liz-nace*
powder becomes *piz-now|diz-ner*
ring becomes *riz-ning*
rubber band becomes *riz-nub|biz-ner biz-nand*
scrunchie becomes *scriz-nun|chiz-nie*
sunglasses becomes *siz-nun|gliz-nas|siz-nes*
watch becomes *wiz-natch*

THE BODY (thiz-ne biz-no|diz-ny)

head becomes *hiz-nead*
ear becomes *iz-near*
eye becomes *iz-neye*
nose becomes *niz-nose*
cheek becomes *chiz-neek*

mouth becomes *miz-nouth*
tooth becomes *tiz-nooth*
teeth becomes *tiz-neeth*
chin becomes *chiz-nin*
neck becomes *niz-neck*
shoulder becomes *shiz-noul|diz-ner*
chest becomes *chiz-nest*
arm becomes *iz-narm*
elbow becomes *iz-nel|biz-now*
wrist becomes *wriz-nist*
hand becomes *hiz-nand*
finger becomes *fiz-in|giz-ner*
thumb becomes *thiz-numb*
back becomes *biz-nack*
chest becomes *chiz-nest*
stomach becomes *stiz-no|miz-nach*
hips becomes *hiz-nips*
butt becomes *biz-nutt*
leg becomes *liz-neg*
knee becomes *kniz-nee*
ankle becomes *iz-nankle*
foot becomes *fiz-noot*
toe becomes *tiz-noe*
beard becomes *biz-neard*
blood becomes *bliz-nood*
bone becomes *biz-none*
brain becomes *briz-nain*
hair becomes *hiz-nair*
heart becomes *hiz-neart*
muscle becomes *miz-nuscle*
mustache becomes *miz-nus|tiz-nache*
nails becomes *niz-nails*
pee becomes *piz-nee*
poop becomes *piz-noop*
skin becomes *skiz-nin*
spit becomes *spiz-nit*

GAMES & SPORTS (giz-names iz-nand spiz-norts)

Airsoft becomes *iz-nair/siz-noft*
archery becomes *iz-nar/chiz-nery*
award becomes *iz-na/wiz-nard*
badminton becomes *biz-nad/miz-nin/tiz-non*
ball becomes *biz-nall*
board game becomes *biz-noard giz-name*
boating becomes *biz-noating*
boxing becomes *biz-noxing*
cards becomes *ciz-nards*
champion becomes *chiz-nampion*
checkers becomes *chiz-nec/kiz-ners*
chess becomes *chiz-ness*
competition becomes *ciz-nom/piz-ne/tiz-nition*
cricket becomes *criz-nic/kiz-net*
diving becomes *diz-niving*
dodgeball becomes *diz-nodge biz-nall*
field hockey becomes *fiz-nield hiz-noc/kiz-ney*
final becomes *fiz-ni/niz-nal*
finish line becomes *fiz-ninish liz-nine*
flag football becomes *fliz-nag fiz-noot/biz-nall*
foul becomes *fiz-noul*
four square becomes *fiz-nour squiz-nare*
game becomes *giz-name*
goal becomes *giz-noal*
golf becomes *giz-nolf*
gymnastics becomes *giz-nym/niz-nas/tiz-nics*
handball becomes *hiz-nand biz-nall*
hang gliding becomes *hiz-nang gliz-niding*
home team becomes *his-nome tiz-neam*
hoops basketball becomes *hiz-noops biz-nas/kiz-net/biz-nall*
hopscotch becomes *hiz-nop/sciz-notch*
horseback riding becomes *his-norse/biz-nack riz-niding*
horseshoes becomes *his-norse shiz-noes*
ice skating becomes *iz-nice skiz-nating*

jacks becomes *jiz-nacks*
jogging becomes *jiz-nogging*
judo becomes *jiz-nu|diz-no*
karate becomes *kiz-na|riz-na|tiz-ne*
kickball becomes *kiz-nick|biz-nall*
kick the can becomes *kiz-nick thiz-ne ciz-nan*
lacrosse becomes *liz-na|criz-nosse*
lawn bowling becomes *liz-nawn biz-nowling*
lose becomes *liz-nose*
marbles becomes *miz-narbles*
Marco Polo becomes *miz-nar|ciz-no piz-no|liz-no*
match becomes *miz-natch*
MMA becomes *miz|miz|iz-na*
paintball becomes *piz-naint|biz-nall*
pétanque becomes *piz-né|tiz-nanque*
ping pong becomes *piz-ning piz-nong*
polo becomes *piz-no|liz-no*
race becomes *riz-nace*
racquetball becomes *riz-nac|quiz-nuet|biz-nall*
referee becomes *riz-ne|fiz-neree*
ribbon becomes *riz-nib|biz-non*
rollerblading becomes *riz-nol|liz-ner|bliz-nading*
round becomes *riz-nound*
rugby becomes *riz-nug|biz-ny*
running becomes *riz-nunning*
sailing becomes *siz-nailing*
score becomes *sciz-nore*
SCUBA diving becomes *sciz-nu|biz-na diz-niving*
shuffleboard becomes *shiz-nuffle biz-noard*
skateboarding becomes *skiz-nate|biz-noarding*
skiing becomes *skiz-niing*
snorkeling becomes *sniz-norkling*
snowboarding becomes *sniz-now|biz-noarding*
soccer becomes *siz-noc|ciz-ner*
swimming becomes *swiz-nimming*
Tae Kwon Do becomes *tiz-nae kwiz-non diz-no*
tag becomes *tiz-nag*
tennis becomes *tiz-nen|niz-nis*

track and field becomes *triz-nack iz-nand fiz-nield*
trophy becomes *triz-no/phiz-ny*
video game becomes *viz-ni/diz-neo giz-name*
visiting team becomes *viz-nis/i/ting tiz-neam*
volleyball becomes *viz-nol/liz-ney/biz-nall*
water polo becomes *wiz-na/tiz-ner piz-no/liz-no*
weight lifting becomes *wiz-neight liz-nifting*
win becomes *wiz-nin*
windsurfing becomes *wiz-nind/siz-nurfing*
wrestling becomes *wriz-nestling*

CONVERSATION (ciz-non|viz-ner|siz-nation)

I don't like football becomes *iz-ni diz-non't liz-nike fiz-noot/biz-nall*

Great. I'm free on Sunday becomes *griz-nate iz-ni'm friz-nee iz-non siz-nun/diz-nay*

Would you like to have lunch? becomes *wiz-nould yiz-nou liz-ni ke tiz-no hiz-nave liz-nunch?*

Perhaps another time becomes *piz-ner/hiz-naps iz-ano/thiz-ner tiz-nime*

What time does the game start? becomes *whiz-nat tiz-nime diz-noes thiz-ne giz- name stiz-nart?*

I'm sorry. What did you say? becomes *iz-ni'm siz-nor/riz-ny. whiz-nat diz-nid yiz-nou siz-nay?*

That's so boring! becomes *thiz-nat's siz-no biz-noring!*

I'm interested in art becomes *iz-ni'm iz-ninter/e/sted iz-nin iz-nart*, and the word *iz-ninter/e/sted* follows Rule Numbers 3 and 6

I like going to the movies becomes *iz-ni liz-nike giz-noing tiz-no* *thiz-ne miz-novies*

He has blue eyes and wears glasses becomes *hiz-ne hiz-nas bliz-nue iz-neyes iz-nand wiz-nears gliz-nas|siz-nes*

VERBS (viz-nerbs)

TO BE (tiz-no biz-ne), which is pronounced *tiz-noo biz-nee*

Present Simple

I am	*iz-ni iz-nam*	we are	*wiz-ne iz-nare*
you are	*yiz-nou yiz-nare*	you are	*yiz-nou iz-nare*
he is	*hiz-ne iz-nis*	they are	*thiz-ney iz-nare*
she is	*shiz-ne iz-nis*		

Past Simple

I was	*iz-ni wiz-nas*	we were	*wiz-ne wiz-nere*
you were	*yiz-nou wiz-nere*	you were	*yiz-nou wiz-nere*
he was	*hiz-ne wiz-nas*	they were	*thiz-ney wiz-nere*
she was	*shiz-ne wiz-nas*		

Future

I will be	*iz-ni wiz-nill biz-ne*	we will be	*wiz-ne wiz-nill biz-ne*
you will be	*yiz-nou wiz-nill biz-ne*	you will be	*yiz-nou wiz-nill biz-ne*
he will be	*hiz-ne wiz-nill biz-ne*	they will be	*thiz-ney wiz-nill biz-ne*
she will be	*shiz-ne wiz-nill biz-ne*		

TO GO (tiz-no giz-no)

Present Simple

I go	*iz-ni giz-no*	we go	*wiz-ne giz-no*
you go	*yiz-nou giz-no*	you go	*yiz-nou giz-no*
he goes	*hiz-ne giz-noes*	they go	*thiz-ney giz-no*
she goes	*shiz-ne giz-noes*		

Past Simple

I went	*iz-ni wiz-nent*	we went	*wiz-ne wiz-nent*
you went	*yiz-nou wiz-nent*	you went	*yiz-nou wiz-nent*
he went	*hiz-ne wiz-nent*	they went	*thiz-ney wiz-nent*
she went	*shiz-ne wiz-nent*		

Future

I will go	*iz-ni wiz-nill giz-no*	we will go	*wiz-ne wiz-nill giz-no*
you will go	*yiz-nou wiz-nill giz-no*	you will go	*yiz-nou wiz-nill giz-no*
he will go	*hiz-ne wiz-nill giz-no*	they will go	*thiz-ney wiz-nill giz-no*
she will go	*shiz-ne wiz-nill giz-no*		

TO HAVE (tiz-no hiz-nave), pronounced *tiz-noo hiz-nav.*

Present Simple

I have	*iz-ni hiz-nave*	we have	*wiz-ne hiz-nave*
you have	*yiz-nou hiz-nave*	you have	*yiz-nou hiz-nave*
he has	*hiz-ne hiz-nas*	they have	*thiz-ney hiz-nave*
she has	*shiz-ne hiz-nas*		

Past Simple

I had	*iz-ni wiz-nad*	we had	*wiz-ne hiz-nad*
you had	*yiz-nou hiz-nad*	you had	*yiz-nou hiz-nad*
he had	*hiz-ne hiz-nad*	they had	*thiz-ney hiz-nad*
she had	*shiz-ne hiz-nad*		

44

Future

I will have   *iz-ni wiz-nill hiz-nave*

you will have *yiz-nou wiz-nill hiz-nave*

he will have   *hiz-ne wiz-nill hiz-nave*

she will have *shiz-ne wiz-nill hiz-nave*

we will have   *wiz-ne wiz-nill hiz-nave*

you will have *yiz-nou wiz-nill hiz-nave*

they will have *thiz-ney wiz-nill hiz-nave*

TO SPEAK (tiz-no spiz-neak)

Present Simple

I speak   *iz-ni spiz-neak*   we speak   *wiz-ne spiz-neak*
you speak   *yiz-nou spiz-neak*   you speak   *yiz-nou spiz-neak*
he speaks   *hiz-ne spiz-neaks*   they speak *thiz-ney spiz-neak*
she speaks *shiz-ne spiz-neak*

Past Simple

I spoke   *iz-ni spiz-noke*   we spoke   *wiz-ne spiz-noke*
you spoke   *yiz-nou spiz-noke*   you spoke   *yiz-nou spiz-noke*
he spoke   *hiz-ne spiz-noke*   they spoke *thiz-ney spiz-noke*
she spoke   *shiz-ne spiz-noke*

Future

I will speak   *iz-ni wiz-nill spiz-neak*   we will speak   *wiz-ne wiz-nill spiz-neak*

you will speak *yiz-nou wiz-nill spiz-neak*   you will speak *yiz-nou wiz-nill spiz-neak*

he will speak   *hiz-ne wiz-nill spiz-neak*   they will speak *thiz-ney wiz-nill spiz-neak*

she will speak *shiz-ne wiz-nill spiz-neak*

TO WANT (tiz-no wiz-nant)

Present Simple

I want	*iz-ni wiz-nant*	we want	*wiz-ne wiz-nant*
you want	*yiz-nou wiz-nant*	you want	*yiz-nou wiz-nant*
he wants	*hiz-ne wiz-nants*	they want	*thiz-ney wiz-nant*
she wants	*shiz-ne wiz-nants*		

Past Simple

I wanted	*iz-ni wiz-nanted*	we wanted	*wiz-ne wiz-nant ed*
you wanted	*yiz-nou wiz-nanted*	you wanted	*yiz-nou wiz-nanted*
he wanted	*hiz-ne wiz-nanted*	they wanted	*thiz-ney wiz-nanted*
she had	*shiz-ne wiz-nanted*		

Future

I will want	*iz-ni wiz-nill wiz-nant*	we will want	*wiz-ne wiz-nill wiz-nant*
you will want	*yiz-nou wiz-nill wiz-nant*	you will want	*yiz-nou wiz-nill wiz-nant*
he will want	*hiz-ne wiz-nill wiz-nant*	they will want	*thiz-ney wiz-nill wiz-nant*
she will want	*shiz-ne wiz-nill wiz-nant*		

READING EXERCISE (riz-neading iz-nexer|-ciz-nise)

twiz-ninkle, twiz-ninkle, liz-nittle stiz-nar,
hiz-now iz-ni wiz-non/diz-ner whiz-nat yiz-nou iz-nare!
iz-nup iz-na/biz-nove thiz-ne wiz-norld siz-no hiz-nigh,
liz-nike iz-na diz-nia/miz-nond iz-nin thiz-ne skiz-ny

What you just read was the popular English lullaby "Twinkle, Twinkle, Little Star."

Twinkle, twinkle, little star,
How I wonder what you are!
Up above the world so high,
Like a diamond in the sky.

riz-ning iz-na|riz-nound thiz-ne riz-nosie,
iz-na piz-noc|kiz-net fiz-nul iz-nof piz-nosies,
iz-nashes iz-nashes
wiz-ne iz-nall fiz-nall diz-nown

This one is the rursery rhyme "Ring Around the Rosie." The common American version goes like this:

Ring around the rosie,
A pocket full of posies,
Ashes! Ashes!
We all fall down.

Now try some classical English literature from Shakespeare's "Romeo and Juliet" written in 1592 (everyone should read his plays).

iz-no riz-no|miz-neo, riz-no|miz-neo! whiz-nere|fiz-nore iz-nart
thiz-nou riz-no|miz-neo?
diz-ne|niz-ny thiz-ny fiz-na|thiz-ner iz-nand riz-ne|fiz-nuse thiz-
ny niz-name;
iz-nor, iz-nif thiz-nou wiz-nilt niz-not, biz-ne biz-nut swiz-norn
miz-ny liz-nove,
iz-nand iz-ni'll niz-no liz-non|giz-ner biz-ne iz-na ciz-nap|u|liz-
net

O Romeo, Romeo! Wherefore art thou Romeo?
Deny thy father and refuse thy name;
Or, if thou wilt not, be but sworn my love,
And I'll no longer be a Capulet.

That was a tough one. Turning modern Engligh into spiz-neak is hard enough. Turning Shakespeare into spiz-neak is really a challenge, but would be a lot of fun for drama students, and one of his plays would would make for a great YouTube video one day.

WRITING EXERCISE (wriz-niting iz-nexer|-ciz-nise)

Read the following questions and then write down the correct anwer in spiz-neak on the line.

1. What is your name?

_____

2. What is the name of your school?

_____

3. What country do you live in?

_____

4. What is your favorite book?

_____

5. How old are you?

_____

6. What is your best friend's name?

_____

7. What is the name of your pet?

8. What is your favorite sport?

9. What is your favorite T.V. show?

TRANSLATION EXERCISE (triz-nans|liz-na-tion)

Translate the following English sentences into spiz-neak. The correct translation will be at the end so that you can check your work.

1. On Thursday I am going with my family to France for vacation.

2. Karen and John went to see the movie last night. I did not go.

3. Our school is going on a field trip next month to the city zoo. I can't wait!

_____

_____

_____

_____

4. Mr. Jones is the best history teacher in the school. I am learning a lot from him.

_____

_____

_____

_____

Answers (iz-nan|swiz-ners)

1. *iz-non thiz-nurs|diz-nay iz-ni iz-nam giz-noing wiz-nith miz-ny fiz-nam|i|liz-ny tiz-no friz-nace fiz-nor viz-na|ciz-nation*

2. *kiz-naren iz-nand jiz-nohn wiz-net tiz-no siz-nee thiz-ne miz-no|viz-nie liz-nast* niz-night. *iz-ni diz-nid niz-not giz-no*

3. *iz-nour schiz-nool iz-nis giz-noing iz-non iz-na fiz-nield triz-nip niz-next miz-nonth tiz-no thiz-ne ciz-ni|tiz-ny ziz-noo. iz-ni ciz-nan't wiz-nait!*

4. *miz-nis|tiz-ner jiz-nones iz-niz thiz-ne biz-nest hiz-nis|tiz-no|riz-ny iz-nin thiz-ne schiz-nool. iz-ni iz-nam liz-nearning iz-na liz-not friz-nom hiz-nim*

VOCABULARY (viz-no|ciz-nab|u|liz-ary)

A

able become *iz-nable*
account becomes *iz-nac|ciz-nount*
accuse becomes *iz-nac|ciz-nuse*
ace becomes *iz-nace*
acne becomes *iz-nac|niz-ne*
across becomes *iz-nacross*
action becomes *iz-naction*
actor becomes *iz-nac|tiz-nor*
add becomes *iz-nadd*
address becomes *iz-nad|driz-ness*
admire becomes *iz-nad|miz-mire*
advice becomes *iz-nad|viz-nice*
after becomes *iz-naf|tiz-ner*
afternoon becomes *iz-naf|tiz-ner|niz-noon*
agent becomes *iz-nagent*
air becomes *iz-nair*
airplane becomes *iz-nair|pliz-nane*
alert becomes *iz-na|liz-nert*
algebra becomes *iz-nal|giz-ne|briz-na*
alphabet becomes *iz-nal|phiz-na|biz-net*
allow becomes *iz-nal|liz-now*
am becomes *iz-nam*
android becomes *iz-nan|driz-noid*
animal becomes *iz-nan|i|miz-nal*
antenna becomes *iz-an|tiz-nenna*
app becomes *iz-napp*
apple becomes *iz-napple*
apologize becomes *iz-na|piz-nol|o|giz-nize*
approach becomes *iz-nap|priz-noach*
area becomes *iz-narea*
army become *iz-narmy*
art becomes *iz-nart*
artist becomes *iz-nartist*

ask becomes *iz-nask*
assume becomes *iz-nas/siz-nume*
ate becomes *iz-nate*
attention becomes *iz-nat/tiz-nention*
audio becomes *iz-nau/diz-nio*
author becomes *iz-nau/thiz-nor*
automatic becomes *iz-nauto-miz-natic*

B

baby becomes *biz-naby*
babysitter becomes *biz-aby/siz-nit/tiz-ner*
back becomes *biz-nack*
backpack becomes *biz-nack/piz-nack*
bad becomes *biz-nad*
balcony becomes *biz-nal/ciz-nony*
ball becomes *biz-nall*
bark becomes *biz-nark*
barrier becomes *biz-nar/riz-nier*
baseball becomes *biz-nase/biz-nall*
basic becomes *biz-na/siz-nic*
basketball becomes *biz-nask/et/biz-nall*
bat becomes *biz-nat*
bath becomes *biz-nath*
bathroom becomes *biz-nath/riz-noom*
battle becomes *biz-nattle*
bay becomes *biz-nay*
beach becomes *biz-neach*
beat becomes *biz-neat*
bed becomes *biz-ned*
bee becomes *biz-nee*
been becomes *biz-neen*
behind becomes *biz-ne/hiz-nind*
belch becomes *biz-nelch*
bell becomes *biz-nell*
belt becomes *biz-nelt*
best becomes *biz-nest*

best friend becomes *biz-nest friz-niend*
better becomes *biz-net|tiz-ner*
big becomes *biz-nig*
bike becomes *biz-nike*
biology becomes *biz-nio|liz-nogy*
bird becomes *biz-nird*
birthday becomes *biz-nirth|diz-nay*
blackboard becomes *bliz-nack|biz-noard*
blanket becomes *bliz-nank|kiz-net*
bleach becomes *bliz-neach*
blow-dry becomes *bliz-now|driz-ny*
boat becomes *biz-noat*
body becomes *biz-no|diz-ny*
book becomes *biz-nook*
bottle becomes *biz-nottle*
bore becomes *biz-nore*
boring becomes *biz-noring*
bounce becomes *biz-nounce*
boy becomes *biz-noy*
boyfriend becomes *biz-noy|friz-nend*
box becomes *biz-nox*
bread becomes *briz-nead*
break becomes *briz-neak*
breakfast becomes *briz-neak|fiz-ast*
bring becomes *briz-ning*
broke becomes *briz-noke*
bounce becomes *biz-nounce*
brush becomes *briz-nush*
budget becomes *biz-nud|giz-net*
bugle becomes *biz-nugle*
building becomes *biz-nuil|diz-ning*
bug becomes *biz-nug*
bully becomes *biz-nully*
burp bececomes *biz-nurp*
bus becomes *biz-nus*
business becomes *biz-nus|i|niz-ness*
busy becomes *biz-nusny*
buy becomes *biz-nuy*

C

cab becomes *ciz-nab*
cactus becomes *ciz-nac/tiz-nus*
cage becomes *ciz-nage*
cake become *ciz-nake*
calendar becomes *ciz-nal/en/diz-nar*
calculator becomes *ciz-nal/ciz-nul/liz-nator*
camera becomes *ciz-nam/era*
camp becomes *ciz-namp*
camping becomes *ciz-namping*
candy becomes *ciz-nandy*
capital becomes *ciz-nap/i/tiz-nal*
car becomes *ciz-nar*
card becomes *ciz-nard*
care becomes *ciz-nare*
cartoon becomes *ciz-nar/tiz-noon*
case becomes *ciz-nase*
cash becomes *ciz-nash*
cashier becomes *ciz-nashier*
cat becomes *ciz-nat*
CD becomes *ciz-nee/diz-nee*
celebration becomes *ciz-nel/e/briz-nation*
center becomes *ciz-nen/tiz-ner*
cents becomes *ciz-nents*
certain becomes *ciz-ner/tiz-nain*
chair becomes *chiz-nair*
charge becomes *chiz-narge*
chase becomes *chiz-nase*
check becomes *chiz-neck*
choice becomes *chiz-noice*
chop becomes *chiz-nop*
clock becomes *cliz-nock*
church becomes *chiz-nurch*
city becomes *ciz-nity*
coat becomes *ciz-noat*
coffee becomes *ciz-nof/fiz-nee*
coin becomes *ciz-noin*

college becomes *ciz-nol|liz-nege*
color becomes *ciz-no|liz-nor*
collect becomes *ciz-nol|liz-nect*
commercial becomes *ciz-nom|miz-ner|ciz-nial*
community becomes *ciz-nom|miz-nunity*
conflict becomes *ciz-non|fliz-nict*
computer becomes *ciz-nom|piz-nuter*
control becomes *ciz-non|triz-nol*
cook becomes *ciz-nook*
cool becomes *ciz-nool*
copy becomes *ciz-nopy*
corner becomes *ciz-nor|niz-ner*
corner becomes *ciz-nor|niz-ner*
couch becomes *ciz-nouch*
count becomes *ciz-nount*
county becomes *ciz-noun|tiz-ny*
country becomes *ciz-noun|triz-ny*
crash becomes *criz-nash*
crayon becomes *criz-nay|iz-non*
crime becomes *criz-nime*
criminal becomes *criz-nim|i|niz-nal*
cup becomes *ciz-nup*
cuss becomes *ciz-nuss*
cut becomes *ciz-nut*
cute becomes *ciz-nute*

D

daily becomes *diz-nai|liz-ny*
danger becomes *diz-nan|giz-ner*
dare becomes *diz-nare*
day becomes *diz-nay*
dead becomes *diz-nead*
deal becomes *diz-neal*
deep becomes *diz-neep*
delete becomes *diz-ne|liz-nete*
delight becomes *diz-ne|liz-night*

delinquent becomes *diz-ne/liz-nin/quiz-nent*
deliver becomes *diz-ne/liz-niver*
demonstrate becomes *diz-nem/on/striz-nate*
deserve becomes *diz-ne/siz-nerve*
desk becomes *diz-nesk*
dessert becomes *diz-nes/siz-nert*
detention becomes *diz-ne/tiz-nention*
dictionary becomes *diz-niction/niz-ary*
diet becomes *diz-niet*
different becomes *diz-nif/fiz-nerent*
difficult becomes *diz-niff/i/ciz-nult*
dig becomes *diz-nig*
dinner becomes *diz-ninner*
disk becomes *diz-nisk*
doctor becomes *diz-noc/tiz-nor*
dog becomes *diz-nog*
dollar becomes *diz-nollar*
don't becomes *diz-non't*
double becomes *diz-nouble*
doubt becomes *diz-noubt*
down becomes *diz-nown*
dish becomes *diz-nish*
dive becomes *diz-nive*
draw becomes *driz-naw*
drawer becomes *driz-nawer*
dress becomes *driz-ness*
drive becomes *driz-nive*
drum becomes *driz-num*
dull becomes *diz-null*
dumb becomes *diz-numb*
dye becomes *diz-nye*

E

early becomes *iz-near/liz-ny*
earth becomes *iz-nearth*
eat becomes *iz-neat*

ecology becomes *iz-ne|ciz-nology*
economics becomes *iz-nec|o|niz-nomics*
egg becomes *iz-negg*
elephant becomes *iz-nel|e|phiz-nant*
elevator becomes *iz-nel|e|viz-nator*
email become *iz-ne|miz-nail*
empty becomes *iz-emp|tiz-ny*
energy becomes *iz-nen|er|giz-ny*
English becomes *iz-nen|gliz-nish*
enjoy becomes *iz-nen|jiz-nly*
enter becomes *iz-nen|triz-ner*
entrance becomes *iz-nen|triz-nance*
envelope becomes *iz-nen|viz-nel|nope*
eraser becomes *iz-ne|riz-naser*
eye becomes *iz-neye*
equal becomes *iz-equal*
Europe becomes *iz-neu|riz-nope*
evening becomes *iz-nevening*
everyone becomes *iz-neve|riz-nyone*
evict becomes *iz-ne|viz-nict*
exam becomes *iz-nex|nam*
example becomes *iz-nex|iz-nample*
exit becomes *iz-nex|nit*
expensive becomes *iz-nex|piz-pen|siz-nive*
extra becomes *iz-nex|triz-na*
extreme becomes *iz-nex|triz-neme*

F

failure becomes *fiz-nailure*
fair becomes *fiz-nair*
false becomes *fiz-nalse*
familiar becomes *fiz-nam|i|liz-niar*
family becomes *fiz-nam|i|liz-ny*
famous becomes *fiz-nam|nous*
fart becomes *fiz-nart*
fat becomes *fiz-nat*

fear becomes *fiz-near*
fight becomes *fiz-night*
file becomes *fiz-nile*
film becomes *fiz-nilm*
finger becomes *fiz-nin/giz-ner*
fire become *fiz-nire*
first becomes *fiz-nirst*
fish becomes *fiz-nish*
fishing becomes *fiz-nishing*
fix becomes *fiz-nix*
flag becomes *fliz-nag*
flee becomes *fliz-nee*
feet becomes *fiz-neet*
flower becomes *fliz-nower*
flute becomes *fliz-nute*
fog becomes *fiz-nog*
folder becomes *fiz-nolder*
food becomes *fiz-nood*
fool becomes *fiz-nool*
foot becomes *fiz-noot*
football becomes *fiz-noot/biz-nall*
force becomes *fiz-norce*
forest becomes *fiz-norest*
forgive becomes *fiz-nor/giz-nive*
fork becomes *fiz-nork*
forward becomes *fiz-nor/wiz-nard*
foundation becomes *fiz-noun/diz-nation*
frame becomes *friz-name*
frat becomes *friz-nat*
fraternity becomes *friz-nat/er/niz-nity*
freeway becomes *friz-nee/wiz-nay*
French becomes *friz-nench*
friend becomes *friz-niend*
fuel becomes *fiz-nuel*
fun becomes *fiz-nun*
funny becomes *fiz-nun/niz-ny*
future becomes *fiz-nu/tiz-nure*

G

game becomes *giz-name*
gang becomes *giz-nang*
garage becomes *giz-na|riz-nage*
gas becomes *giz-nas*
gate becomes *giz-nate*
geography becomes *giz-neo|griz-naphy*
general becomes *giz-nen|e|riz-nal*
generous becomes *giz-nen|erous*
German becomes *giz-ner|miz-nan*
get becomes *giz-net*
gift becomes *giz-nift*
girl becomes *giz-nirl*
girlfriend becomes *giz-nirl|friz-nend*
glad becomes *gliz-nad*
globe becomes *gliz-nobe*
glue becomes *gliz-nue*
go becomes *giz-no*
gold becomes *giz-nold*
golf becomes *giz-nolf*
good becomes *giz-nood*
gone becomes *giz-none*
grade becomes *griz-nade*
greasy becomes *griz-nea|siz-ny*
great becomes *griz-neat*
grid becomes *griz-nid*
group become *griz-noup*
guard becomes *guiz-nard*
guide becomes *guiz-nide*
guitar becomes *guiz-ni|tiz-nar*
gum becomes *giz-num*
gun becomes *giz-nun*
gut becomes *giz-nut*
guy becomes *giz-nuy*
gym becomes *gyiz-n'm*
gymnastics becomes *gyiz-n'm|niz-nas|tiz-nics*

H

hair becomes *hiz-nair*
hairdresser becomes *hiz-nair/driz-nes/siz-ner*
hairspray becomes *hiz-nair/spriz-nay*
hammer becomes *hiz-nam/miz-ner*
hamster becomes *hiz-nam/stiz-ner*
happy becomes *hiz-nappy*
harsh becomes *hiz-narsh*
has becomes *his-nas*
hat becomes *hiz-nat*
hate becomes *hiz-nate*
have becomes *hiz-nave*
he becomes *hiz-ne*
health becomes *hiz-nealth*
heat becomes *hiz-neat*
helicopter becomes *hiz-nel/i/ciz-nop/tiz-ner*
her becomes *hiz-ner*
highway becomes *hiz-nigh/wiz-nay*
hike becomes *hiz-nike*
hiking becomes *hiz-niking*
him becomes *hiz-nim*
history becomes *hiz-nis/tiz-no/riz-ny*
hit becomes *hiz-nit*
hockey becomes *hiz-noc/kiz-ney*
hole becomes *hiz-nole*
home becomes *hiz-nome*
hoop becomes *hiz-noop*
hope becomes *hiz-nope*
hot becomes *hiz-not*
hotel becomes *hiz-no/tiz-nel*
horror becomes *hiz-nor/riz-nor*
horse becomes *his-norse*
house becomes *hiz-nouse*
huge becomes *hiz-nuge*
humor becomes *hiz-nu/miz-nor*
hurry becomes *hiz-nurry*
husband becomes *hiz-nus/biz-nand*

I

I becomes *iz-ni*
ice becomes *iz-nice*
idea becomes *iz-ni|diz-nea*
ideal becomes *iz-ni|diz-neal*
important becomes *iz-nim|piz-nortant*
index becomes *iz-nin|diz-nex*
ink becomes *iz-nink*
intelligent becomes *iz-nintel|liz-nigent*
interesting becomes *iz-ninter|resting*
invitation becomes *iz-nin|viz-ni|tiz-nation*
iPad becomes *iz-ni|piz-nad*
iPhone becomes *iz-ni|phiz-none*
iron becomes *iz-ni|riz-on*
ironic becomes *iz-ni|riz-nonic*
iTunes becomes *iz-ni|tiz-nunes*
it becomes *iz-nit*

J

jacket becomes *jiz-nac|kiz-net*
jail becomes *jiz-nail*
jet becomes *jiz-net*
join becomes *jiz-noin*
joke becomes *jiz-noke*
joy becomes *jiz-noy*
juice becomes *jiz-nuice*
jump becomes *jiz-nump*
June become *jiz-nune*
just become *jiz-nust*
justice becomes *jiz-nus|tiz-nice*

K

keep becomes *kiz-neep*
key becomes *kiz-ney*

keyboard becomes *kiz-ney/biz-noard*
kid becomes *kiz-nid*
kilo becomes *kiz-nilo*
kilometer becomes *kiz-ni/liz-no/miz-neter*
kind becomes *kiz-nind*
king becomes *kiz-ning*
kiss becomes *kiz-niss*
kite becomes *kiz-nite*
knife becomes *kniz-nife*

L

lake becomes *liz-nake*
lamp becomes *liz-namp*
last becomes *liz-nast*
late become *liz-nate*
laugh becomes *liz-naugh*
laundry becomes *liz-aun/driz-ny*
lazy becomes *liz-na/zy*
leaf becomes *liz-neaf*
learn becomes *liz-nearn*
liar becomes *liz-niar*
liberty becomes *liz-ni/biz-nerty*
liar becomes *liz-niar*
lie becomes *liz-nie*
lift becomes *liz-nift*
light becomes *liz-night*
like becomes *liz-nike*
liquid becomes *liz-ni/quiz-nid*
list becomes *liz-nist*
listen becomes *liz-nistnen*
local becomes *liz-no/ciz-nal*
locker becomes *liz-noc/kiz-ner*
look becomes *liz-nook*
lotion becomes *liz-notion*
loud becomes *liz-noud*
love becomes *liz-nove*

luggage becomes *liz-nug|giz-nage*
lunch becomes *liz-nunch*

M

mail becomes *miz-nail*
make-up becomes *miz-nake|iz-nup*
man becomes *miz-nan*
manicure becomes *miz-nan|i|ciz-nure*
map becomes *miz-nap*
marker becomes *miz-narker*
married becomes *miz-nar|riz-ned*
material becomes *miz-na|tiz-nerial*
math becomes *miz-nath*
measure becomes *miz-nea|siz-nure*
media becomes *miz-ned|nia*
medical becomes *miz-ned|i|ciz-nal*
medicine becomes *miz-ned|i|ciz-nine*
memory becomes *miz-ne|miz-nory*
menu becomes *miz-nenu*
message become *miz-nes|siz-nage*
microwave becomes *miz-ni|criz-no|wiz-nave*
middle becomes *miz-nid|diz-nle*
mike becomes *miz-nike*
milk becomes *miz-nilk*
mine becomes *miz-nine*
mission becomes *miz-nission*
money becomes *miz-noney*
monster becomes *miz-non|stiz-ner*
more becomes *miz-nore*
mosque becomes *miz-nosque*
mountain becomes *miz-noun|tiz-nain*
mouse becomes *miz-nouse*
move becomes *miz-nove*
movie becomes *miz-no|viz-nie*
music becomes *miz-nu|siz-nic*
mystery becomes *mys-iz|tiz-nery*

N

nail becomes *niz-nail*
name becomes *niz-name*
nap becomes *niz-nap*
napkin becomes *niz-nap/kiz-nin*
nation becomes *niz-nation*
neighborhood becomes *niz-neigh/biz-nor/hiz-nood*
necessary becomes *niz-nec/e/ssiz-nary*
next becomes *niz-next*
night becomes *niz-night*
no becomes *niz-no*
noon becomes *niz-noon*
none becomes *niz-none*
not becomes *niz-not*
notebook becomes *niz-note/biz-nook*
note becomes *niz-notes*
nothing becomes *niz-no/thiz-ning*
nurse becomes *niz-nurse*

O

oily becomes *iz-noi/liz-ny*
open becomes *iz-no/piz-nen*
original becomes *iz-nor/i/giz-nial*
out becomes *iz-nout*
outstanding becomes *iz-nout/stiz-nan/diz-ning*
over becomes *iz-no/viz-ner*
overnight becomes *iz-no/viz-ner/niz-night*

P

package becomes *piz-nack/iz-nage*
pain becomes *piz-nain*
paint becomes *piz-naint*
pancake becomes *piz-nan/ciz-nake*

pants becomes *piz-nants*
paper becomes *piz-naper*
party becomes *piz-narty*
paste becomes *piz-naste*
pen becomes *piz-nen*
people becomes *piz-neople*
perfect becomes *piz-ner|fiz-nect*
perform becomes *piz-ner|fiz-norm*
perfume becomes *piz-ner|fiz-nume*
period becomes *piz-ner|iod*
permission becomes *piz-ner|miz-nission*
person becomes *piz-ner|siz-non*
personal becomes *piz-ner|siz-nonal*
phone becomes *phiz-none*
photo becomes *phiz-noto*
phrase becomes *phriz-nase*
physical becomes *physiz-nical*
pity becomes *piz-nity*
plate becomes *pliz-nate*
play becomes *pliz-nay*
playground becomes *pliz-nay|griz-nound*
please becomes *pliz-nease*
plot becomes *pliz-not*
plug becomes *pliz-nug*
poem becomes *piz-noem*
point becomes *piz-noint*
pole becomes *piz-nole*
polite becomes *piz-no|liz-nite*
political becomes *piz-no|liz-nit|i|ciz-nal*
pool becomes *piz-nool*
poor becomes *piz-noor*
popular becomes *piz-nop|u|liz-nar*
possible becomes *piz-nos|siz-nible*
post card becomes *piz-nost ciz-nard*
post office becomes *piz-not iz-nof|fiz-nice*
pound becomes *piz-nound*
practice becomes *priz-nac|tiz-nice*
president becomes *priz-nes|i|diz-nent*

pretty becomes *priz-netty*
price becomes *priz-nice*
printer becomes *priz-nin/tiz-ner*
prison becomes *priz-niz/siz-non*
private becomes *priz-niv/ate*
probable becomes *priz-nob/able*
problem becomes *priz-nob/liz-nem*
professional becomes *priz-no/fiz-nes/siz-nional*
professor becomes *priz-no/fiz-nes/siz-nor*
protest becomes *priz-no/tiz-nest*
purse becomes *piz-nurse*

Q

queen becomes *quiz-neen*
question becomes *quiz-nes/tion*
quiet becomes *quiz-niet*
quit becomes *quiz-nit*

R

rabbit becomes *riz-nab/biz-nit*
race becomes *riz-nace*
radio becomes *riz-na/diz-nio*
rain becomes *riz-nain*
ranch becomes *riz-nanch*
range becomes *riz-nange*
regular becomes *riz-neg/u/liz-nar*
religious becomes *riz-ne/liz-nigious*
repeat becomes *riz-ne/piz-neat*
reservation becomes *riz-nes/er/viz-nation*
responsible becomes *riz-nes/spiz-non/siz-nible*
restaurant becomes *riz-nes/tiz-nau/riz-nant*
review becomes *riz-ne/viz-niew*
rich becomes *riz-nich*
right becomes *riz-night*

room becomes *riz-noom*
rose becomes *riz-nose*
ruler becomes *riz-nuler*
run becomes *riz-nun*

S

sail becomes *siz-nail*
sailing becomes *siz-nailing*
safe becomes *siz-nafe*
sale becomes *siz-nale*
screen becomes *scriz-neen*
sea becomes *siz-nea*
security becomes *siz-nec/u/riz-nity*
secret becomes *siz-ne/criz-net*
self becomes *siz-nelf*
service becomes *siz-ner/viz-nice*
school becomes *schiz-nool*
scissors becomes *scisz-n'sors*
second becomes *siz-ne/ciz-nond*
shampoo becomes *shiz-nam/piz-noo*
shave becomes *shiz-nave*
ship becomes *shiz-nip*
shirt becomes *shiz-nirt*
shock becomes *shiz-nock*
shoe becomes *shiz-noe*
shop becomes *shiz-nop*
shopping becomes *shiz-nop/piz-ning*
shower becomes *shiz-nower*
side becomes *siz-nide*
sign becomes *siz-nign*
single becomes *siz-ningle*
silver becomes *siz-nil/viz-ner*
similar becomes *siz-nim/i/liz-nar*
simple becomes *siz-nimple*
sing becomes *siz-ning*
single becomes *siz-ingle*

slap becomes *sliz-nap*
sleep becomes *sliz-neep*
small becomes *smiz-nall*
smile becomes *smiz-nile*
snack becomes *sniz-nack*
snow becomes *sniz-now*
so becomes *siz-no*
soap becomes *siz-noap*
soccer becomes *siz-noc/ciz-ner*
socialize becomes *siz-no/cialize*
social media becomes *siz-no/ciz-nial miz-ne/diz-nia*
sock becomes *siz-nock*
sorry becomes *siz-nor/riz-ny*
Spanish becomes *spiz-nanish*
spill becomes *spiz-nill*
spin becomes *spiz-nin*
split becomes *spliz-nit*
spoil becomes *spiz-noil*
spoon becomes *spiz-noon*
sport becomes *spiz-nort*
stair becomes *stiz-nair*
stamp becomes *stiz-namp*
star becomes *stiz-nar*
steep becomes *stiz-neep*
stone becomes *stiz-none*
stop becomes *stiz-nop*
story becomes *stiz-nory*
stripes becomes *striz-nipes*
stuff becomes *stiz-nuff*
stupid becomes *stiz-nupid*
succeed becomes *siz-nuc/ciz-need*
success becomes *siz-nuc/ciz-ness*
supply becomes *siz-nup/pliz-ny*
support becomes *siz-nup/piz-nort*
swim becomes *swiz-nim*
swimming becomes *swiz-nim/miz-ning*
switch becomes *swiz-nitch*
synagogue becomes *syniz/a/giz-nogue*

T

tape becomes *tiz-nape*
taxi becomes *tiz-naxi*
teacher becomes *tiz-nea/chiz-ner*
tennis becomes *tiz-nen/niz-nis*
tent becomes *tiz-nent*
test becomes *tiz-nest*
theater becomes *thiz-ne/a/tiz-ner*
theory becomes *thiz-neory*
think becomes *thiz-nink*
thought becomes *thiz-nought*
tip becomes *tiz-nip*
tire becomes *tiz-nire*
tired becomes *tiz-nired*
tissue becomes *tiz-ni/shiz-nue*
tip becomes *tiz-nip*
to becomes *tiz-no*
today becomes *tiz-no/diz-nay*
tone becomes *tiz-none*
tonight becomes *tiz-no/niz-night*
tooth becomes *tiz-nooth*
toothbrush becomes *tiz-nooth/briz-nush*
tool becomes *tiz-nool*
top becomes *tiz-nop*
total becomes *tiz-no/tiz-nal*
touch becomes *tiz-nouch*
towel becomes *tiz-nowel*
town becomes *tiz-nown*
toy becomes *tiz-noy*
train becomes *triz-nain*
trash becomes *triz-nash*
travel becomes *triz-na/viz-nel*
traveling becomes *triz-na/viz-neling*
trick becomes *triz-nick*
through becomes *thriz-nough*
truck becomes *triz-nuck*
true becomes *triz-nue*

trust becomes *triz-nust*
T-shirt becomes *tiz-nee/shiz-nirt*
TV becomes *tiz-nee/viz-nee*

U

ugly becomes i*z-nug/liz-ny*
up becomes *iz-nup*
update becomes *iz-nup/diz-nate*
understand becomes *iz-ni iz-nunder/stiz-nand*
uniform becomes *iz-nuni/fiz-norm*
university becomes *iz-uni/viz-ner/siz-nity*
uptight becomes *iz-nup/tiz-night*
until becomes *iz-nuntil*
unwrap becomes *iz-nunwrap*
USB becomes *iz-nusb*
us becomes *iz-nus*
usual becomes *iz-nusual*

V

van becomes *viz-nan*
very becomes *viz-ne/riz-ny*
victim becomes *viz-nic/tiz-nim*
victory becomes *viz-nic/tiz-nory*
video becomes *viz-ni/diz-neo*
video game becomes *viz-ni/diz-neo giz-name*
view becomes *viz-new*
village becomes *viz-nil/liz-nage*
violin becomes *viz-ni/o/liz-nin*
violence becomes *viz-ni/o/liz-nence*
visit becomes *viz-nisit*
visitor becomes *viz-nis/i/tiz-nor*
voice becomes *viz-noice*
vomit becomes *viz-no/miz-nit*
vote becomes *viz-note*

W

wagon becomes *wiz-na|giz-non*
wait becomes *wiz-nait*
waiter becomes *wiz-nai|tiz-ner*
waitress becomes *wiz-nai|triz-ness*
walk becomes *wiz-nalk*
wall becomes *wiz-nall*
wallet becomes *wiz-nal|liz-net*
wash becomes *wiz-nash*
water becomes *wiz-na|tiz-ner*
we becomes *wiz-ne*
weak becomes *wiz-neak*
weather becomes *wiz-neather*
wet becomes *wiz-net*
why becomes *whiz-ny*
wife becomes *wiz-nife*
wi-fi becomes *wiz-ni|fiz-ni*
wind becomes *wiz-nind*
window becomes *wiz-in|diz-now*
wire becomes *wiz-nire*
wish becomes *wiz-nish*
woman becomes *wiz-no|miz-nan*
wonder becomes *wiz-non|diz-ner*
worse becomes *wiz-norse*
write becomes *wriz-nite*
wrong becomes *wriz-nong*

X

x-ray becomes *iz-nx|riz-nay*

Y

yard becomes *yiz-nard*
yes becomes *yiz-nes*
yesterday becomes *yiz-nes|tiz-ner|diz-nay*

young becomes *yiz-noung*
youth becomes *yiz-nouth*

Z

zebra becomes *ziz-ne|briz-na*
zipper becomes *ziz-nipper*
zombie becomes *ziz-nom|biz-nie*

YOUR OWN VOCABULARY WORDS (yiz-nour iz-nown viz-no|ciz-nab|u|liz-ary wiz-nords)

_____

_____

_____

_____

_____

_____

_____

_____

_____

THE HISTORY OF spiz-neak (thiz-ne hiz-nis|tiz-nory iz-nof spiz-neak)

I did not create the concept of spiz-neak (speak), but I am the foremost authority on spiz-neak. I'm the one who codeified this "dead language" (a language that nobody speaks anymore), and brought it back to "life" so that it could be spoken again.

I first heard this secret language in the mid 1990s when I was a patrol police officer just south of Los Angeles, California. Yes, I know, I am ancient. I heard spiz-neak, although they didn't have a name for it back then, from time to time from some of the criminals I had arrested and brought to jail. That's right, "criminals." Not many of them spoke it, but a few did, which was probably less than 1%.

I have to admit that I could never figure out what these criminals, who spoke spiz-neak, were saying. I strained my ears trying to pick it up, as did many other police officers listening to them, but it was impossible. Of course, I knew it was based on English, like Pig Latin. Pig Latin is a language game that has been around since at least the 1700s, but it is much more difficult to learn and to speak than spiz-neak. There are other language games in English, about 12 of them, but at the time of the printing of this book there was nothing even close to spiz-neak on WIKIPEDIA. The fact was that I didn't know how the criminals were changing the English words.

Then one day I had my big break. I had arrested a young woman who spoke spiz-neak. Although she had committed a crime, and she had to pay for her crime, she seemed to be a nice person.

Because she was friendly I asked her, "Will you tell me how your language works?"

Her answer to me was, "No. I can't do that. I'll get in trouble by the others." The "others" she was talking about were fellow criminals that she knew. Of course, criminals are very secretive, and they don't trust the police.

Just before I was to transport her to the Women's Jail, a twenty minute drive away, she asked me if she could make another phone call.

I told her, "No."

By law American citizens who are arrested by the police are allowed two phone calls within a reasonable time of arrest, and I had already given her the two required phone calls.

The young woman pleaded with me, "Please, I need to make one more call."

I saw my opportunity, and I made her an offer. "I'll give you two more phone calls if you teach me the grammar rules to that strange language I heard you speaking to your friend when I arrested you."

She hesitated, and then finally agreed by saying, "Yes, I'll explain it to you."

Obviously I needed this information so that I could listen in on the conversations of future criminals who spoke this language.

Keeping her word, the woman taught me the grammar rules, and I copied down everything she said to me on the back of some blank Pre-booking/Medical Screening Information forms right there in the jail as she was in the booking cage. After years of trying to unlock the secrets of spiz-neak with no success, this moment was equivelent to finding the Rosetta Stone (this is the stone found by one of Napoleon's soldiers, Pierre-François Bouchard, in 1799 that provided the key to understanding ancient Egyptian hieroglyphs, which could not be read for centuries up until then).

It had worked. When I arrested other criminals who spoke spiz-neak I overheard their conversations, but they thought that I didn't understand them. I never revealed to a single criminal that I understood their language.

As the years passed in my career I noticed that less and less criminals were speaking spiz-neak, unitil I didn't hear it at all anymore from anyone. I was a lawman for many years after that, and the language had completely vanished.

However, spiz-neak never completely died out, for it was during the early 2000s, thanks to the Internet, that I discovered that a few people were using the language; bits and pieces of it anyway. It was not just confined to the criminal world as I had once thought. The three or four times I saw a few spiz-neak sentences posted on social media I noticed that each time it was written differently. It appeared that there were no established grammar rules. Shortly after that time spiz-neak disappeared again. The flame had gone out.

Then an idea came to me in the winter of 2015. For a little fun I started to teach my goddaughters (Darya, Yasmin, and Sanam), who were all teenagers, how to speak spiz-neak. Next I taught my twelve-year-old nephew Gary, and my eleven-year-old niece Manique. They liked it also. In fact, even the adults in the family who watched me teaching them wanted to give it a try. Having such fun with it, I decided to pull out my old police notes on spiz-neak that I had jotted down when I was a police officer, and I breathed new life into spiz-neak. I formalized all of the old rules that I had learned from the woman who had first revealed them to me, and I added some of my own rules, which I have numbered, so that spiz-neak would be easier to learn, easy to teach, and be standardized in the English speaking countries.

Although spiz-neak is fun to speak, especially in front of people you don't want to understand your conversation with the person you are speaking with, keep in mind that speaking another language in front of others who don't understand it is considered rude. If someone who is listening to you speak it asks you to stop, especially a parent or a teacher, you should stop. You want to be polite. On the other hand, if you are in any kind of danger, and you need to warn the person you are talking to of some kind of harm, then this is a situation where spiz-neak is not only useful, but necessary.

I am no longer a police officer, and one of the things I do now is teach people self-defense. On January 21, 2003 I created the Jim Wagner Reality-Based Personal Protection system, and I have taught it on every continent in the world except Antartica. Perhaps one day I'll be invited to go down there to teach a research team. Ha!

I believe that everyone should learn self-defense: young, old, and everyone in between. The martial arts are good for your health, it makes your mind think strategically, it helps you with situational awareness (the ability to recognize potential danger), and if someone tries to harm you or a loved one you might just be able to save yourself or someone you are protecting. Unfortunately, there are many bad people in this world who use violence as a "tool" to get what they want: put fear into people, take something from them, or even hurt them.

Many people, even young people, go to my popular YouTube channel **jimwagnerrbpp** to learn my self-defense techniques and training methods. After all, I have trained some of the top military and police units in the world, and a whole lot of civilians as well. If you do learn from me, or other qualified instructors, you must always remember to be responsible with your martial arts skills. That means having respect for yourself (no alcohol, no drugs, and no gangs), respecting others, obeying all rules and laws, and using self-defense only as the last resort (when you have no choice). And, if you do use it then you use only the level of force that is legal to do so.

You may want to tell your parents about my book titled *Protecting Others: Self-Defense Strategies and Tactics for Third-Party Protection* published by Black Belt Books. It's for families, and every family should have a copy of it at home or on their device. In it you and your family will learn how to survive many different types of criminal and terrorist attacks, and it even shows step-by-step how to survive a school shooting. You'll see my nephew Gary and my niece Manique, when they were smaller, demonstrating what to do in that situation. It is sad that you should even have to know about such horrible attacks, but this is the world we live in today. It is better to know Reality-Based Personal Protection and not need it than to need it and not know it.

Have fun with spiz-neak, and as I always say to my Reality-Based students – Be A Hard Target (it's a military term which means don't be an easy victim for the bad guys). **Jim Wagner**

Jiz-nim Wiz-nag|niz-ner iz-niz thiz-ne diz-nean iz-nof spiz-neak

CERTIFICATES (ciz-ner|tiz-nif|i|ciz-nates)

Here are your certificates. The first person to introduce spiz-neak to a friend, or anyone for that matter, is called a "speak founder," or in spiz-neak, a **spiz-neak fiz-noun|diz-ner**. "Introduce" means that they know the 8 Rules of spiz-neak. So, if you introduce somebody to the spiz-neak secret language you are the spiz-neak fiz-noun|diz-ner, and you sign your name on the top of the first certificate. Whoever is the person you introduced it to then signs their name on the second line. To remember this historic moment you will write the date on the last line of the certificate. Keep the certificate in this book, as a permanent record, and it will be fun to look back at it years from now.

If you manage to get three to six people together, who all have the ability to to communicate in spiz-neak with one another (although it does not have to be fluent or the lingua franca - a good phrase to look up - that replaces English each time you get together), that is called a "speak club," or more accurately a **spiz-neak cliz-nub**. If you are the speaz-neak founder of this club you are to sign your name at the top of this certificate. Or, you may be joining another group of people, in which case that spiz-neak founder will sign his or her name at the top of the certificate. It is whoever is the spiz-neak founder of that club. Yes, they may have their own **spiz-neak** book, but everyone in the club signs each other's books. Years from now you don't want to forget who was in your club, and it will bring back good memories.

When there are 10 people or more people that communicate with each other in spiz-neak in the same school, or in the neighborhood, that is known as a "speak group," or **spiz-neak griz-noup**. That is the highest level you can go, and it is quite an accomplishment. It shows real leadership from the spiz-neak founder, and therefore their name goes on the top line. The rest of the members sign on the ten lines below. Some of those signing that certificate could be individuals who were also in the club, or they could be brand new members.

Any amount over 10 people in the same school or neighborhood is known as a "speak community," or **spiz-neak ciz-nom|miz-nuni|tiz-ny**, but there is no certificate for that. It just means that your club became very successful, or there were a lot of other like-minded people in your area with the same idea at the same time. Giz-nood liz-nuck!

ciz-ner|tiz-nif|i|ciz-nate iz-nof iz-nachieve|miz-nent

thiz-nis iz-nis tiz-no ciz-nert|i|fiz-ny thiz-nat

---

siz-nig|niz-na|tiz-nure iz-nof thiz-ne fiz-noun|diz-ner hiz-nere

iz-niz hiz-nere|biz-ny riz-ne|ciz-nog|niz-nized iz-nas iz-na

spiz-neak
fiz-noun|diz-ner

fiz-nor hiz-naving iz-nintro|diz-nuced
thiz-nis siz-ne|criz-net liz-nan|guiz-nage tiz-no

---

siz-nig|niz-na|tiz-nure iz-nof thiz-ne fiz-noun|diz-ner's fiz-nirst stiz-nu|diz-nent hiz-nere

iz-non thiz-nis diz-nay iz-nof

---

diz-nate iz-nof iz-nintro|diz-nuction hiz-nere

siz-nig|niz-na|tiz-nure iz-nof jiz-nim wiz-nag|niz-ner
diz-nean iz-nof spiz-neak

79

ciz-ner|tiz-nif|i|ciz-nate iz-nof iz-nachieve|miz-nent

thiz-nis iz-nis tiz-no ciz-nert|i|fiz-ny thiz-nat

---

siz-nig|niz-na|tiz-nure iz-nof thiz-ne fiz-noun|diz-ner hiz-nere

hiz-nas fiz-normed iz-na

spiz-neak cliz-nub

wiz-nith thiz-ne fiz-nol|liz-nowing miz-nem|biz-ners

---

siz-nig|niz-na|tiz-nure hiz-nere

---

siz-nig|niz-na|tiz-nure hiz-nere

---

siz-nig|niz-na|tiz-nure hiz-nere

---

siz-nig|niz-na|tiz-nure hiz-nere

---

siz-nig|niz-na|tiz-nure hiz-nere

---

siz-nig|niz-na|tiz-nure hiz-nere

thiz-nat biz-ne|giz-nan iz-non

---

diz-nate thiz-ne cliz-nub biz-ne|giz-nan hiz-nere (iz-nonce thiz-nere iz-nis thriz-nee)

iz-nof|iz-nicial
spiz-neak

Siz-nim

siz-nig|niz-na|tiz-nure iz-nof jiz-nim wiz-nag|niz-ner
diz-nean iz-nof spiz-neak

81

ciz-ner|tiz-nif|i|ciz-nate iz-nof iz-nachieve|miz-nent

thiz-nis iz-nis tiz-no ciz-nert|i|fiz-ny thiz-nat

---

siz-nig|niz-na|tiz-nure iz-nof thiz-ne fiz-noun|diz-ner hiz-nere

hiz-nas griz-nown tiz-no thiz-ne liz-nevel iz-nof iz-a

spiz-neak griz-noup

wiz-nith thiz-ne fiz-nol|liz-nowing miz-nem|biz-ners

---
siz-nig|niz-na|tiz-nure hiz-nere

---
siz-nig|niz-na|tiz-nure hiz-nere

---
siz-nig|niz-na|tiz-nure hiz-nere

---
siz-nig|niz-na|tiz-nure hiz-nere

---
siz-nig|niz-na|tiz-nure hiz-nere

---
siz-nig|niz-na|tiz-nure hiz-nere

---
siz-nig|niz-na|tiz-nure hiz-nere

---
siz-nig|niz-na|tiz-nure hiz-nere

---
siz-nig|niz-na|tiz-nure hiz-nere

---
siz-nig|niz-na|tiz-nure hiz-nere

thiz-nat wiz-nas ciz-nom|pliz-neted iz-on

---

diz-nate thiz-nat thiz-ne tiz-nenth miz-nem|biz-ner siz-nigned thiz-nis diz-noc|u|miz-nent

siz-nim

---
siz-nig|niz-na|tiz-nure iz-nof jiz-nim wiz-nag|niz-ner
diz-nean iz-nof spiz-neak